NEBRASKA POW CAMPS

NEBRASKA POW CAMPS

A HISTORY OF WORLD WAR II PRISONERS IN THE HEARTLAND

MELISSA AMATEIS MARSH

THE
History
PRESS

Published by The History Press
Charleston, SC 29403
www.historypress.net

Copyright © 2014 by Melissa Amateis Marsh
All rights reserved

First published 2014

Manufactured in the United States

ISBN 978.1.62619.419.9

Library of Congress Cataloging-in-Publication Data

Marsh, Melissa Amateis.
Nebraska POW camps : a history of World War II prisoners in the heartland / Melissa
Amateis Marsh.
pages cm
Includes bibliographical references and index.
ISBN 978-1-62619-419-9
1. World War, 1939-1945--Prisoners and prisons, American. 2. World War,
1939-1945--Nebraska. 3. Prisoners of war--United States--History--20th century. 4.
Prisoners of war--Germany--History--20th century. 5. Nebraska--History, Military. I. Title.
D805.U5M37 2014
940.54'727309782--dc23
2014009996

Dedicated to those who preserve the past.

CONTENTS

PREFACE

Telling the story of Nebraska's World War II POW camps isn't an easy one. Information for some camps is plentiful, while others are scarce, leaving several gaping holes in the historical record. This is one of the hazards of trying to resurrect the past—too many others were not concerned with *preserving* the past. Files were misplaced, accidentally lost or purposely destroyed. Some camps hardly rated a mention in the town newspaper while other local journalists meticulously recorded the activities at the camp in their community. Each camp's story, therefore, is unique.

You'll notice that I have taken a somewhat unorthodox approach in telling the history of these camps. *Nebraska POW Camps* is neither a scholarly study nor a general history but a mixture of both. I took this route not only because of the scarcity of historical records but also because I tend to have one foot planted in the academic world while the other is firmly in the general, or "popular," world of history. Thus, the book is tailored to both audiences.

Though I would dearly love to treat each camp's story equally, the historical record makes this impossible. Instead, for this book, I focus chiefly on the three base camps of Nebraska—Fort Robinson, Camp Scottsbluff and Camp Atlanta—and then I offer a brief profile on each branch camp. Where possible, I have included anecdotes along with the historical record, though I could not include all due to space reasons.

I hope you will enjoy this look into a time of Nebraska's World War II history that has largely been lost.

ACKNOWLEDGEMENTS

First and foremost: I thank God for giving me the guidance, wisdom and strength to tackle this project.

There are many people to thank, both personally and professionally, for their help and support. For research assistance: Tom Buecker, Sandra Slater, Katie Bradshaw, Allison Young, Bill Baumbach and all those who I spoke with or received letters from reminiscing about their experiences. For graphics and photo help: Katie Nieland, Dave Frank, Jason Ortiz and Randy Bright. For my family both near and far, who have always loved me unconditionally and supported my passion for history: thank you for always being there.

I'd especially like to thank my husband and my daughter for putting up with my long hours at the computer and my vacant gazes when I'm lost in thought and for allowing paperwork and books to clutter nearly every room in the house.

And of course, I couldn't have done it without my three research assistants, aka the cats: Kathryn, LuLu and Slick.

INTRODUCTION

E very summer morning in the early 1940s, Lois Neeley's mother would head to the strawberry patch on their family farm five miles northeast of Scottsbluff, Nebraska. There she met her neighbor, and the two women would fill their pails with strawberries. Lois's mother put those strawberries to good use. Though she froze most of them, she made plenty of strawberry jam, strawberry pie and even strawberry ice cream. For her, there was never too much of strawberry anything. After her foray into the strawberry patch, she would make a large sheet cake perfect for strawberry shortcake.

And one day, she used six servings of strawberry shortcake to break the rules.

"There were strict rules the farmer had to follow when using POWs," Lois remembers. Her father needed help to build a large shed to store winter farm implements. He asked for permission to use POW labor from the nearby POW camp in Scottsbluff. The minimum number of POWs they could have was six, and that's how many he picked up from the camp at 6:00 a.m. Lois's father loaded them into the back of his pickup and headed for the farm. No guard accompanied them.

But there were still procedures to follow—important ones. After all, this was the *enemy*. "They were not to be given any food," Lois recalls, "[and you could] never allow them in your yard to sit on the grass and above all, never invite them into your home." Lois's father talked to other area farmers, who assured him that no camp guards came out and checked to make sure those rules were being followed. He planned to follow them from the get-go. Except…

POW Camps in Nebraska duri

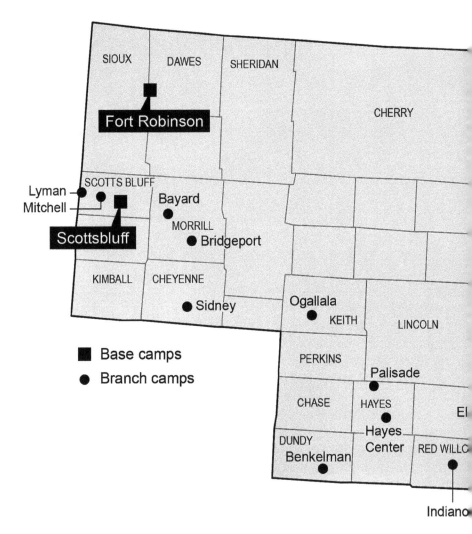

This map shows the locations of POW camps in Nebraska during World War II. *Map designed by Katie Nieland.*

"Each prisoner was given a sack lunch for their noon meal, which consisted of one or two slices of stale dry bread, one slice of stale lunchmeat and a thermos of strong black coffee," Lois said. "After all, they were prisoners

14

d War II

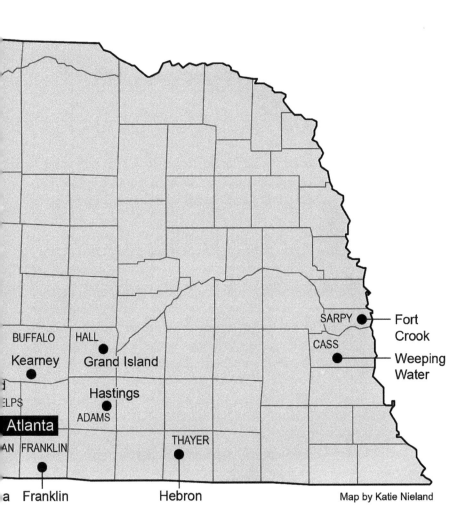

Map by Katie Nieland

and had to be treated like prisoners." Bread, lunchmeat and coffee were a little bit better than the standard fare of bread and water, but surely it didn't satisfy these men's appetites.

So Lois's parents made a decision. "We had a large fenced-in yard with lots of grass and shade trees," Lois said. "Dad let the prisoners sit on the grass to eat their sack lunches." That was one rule violated. But Lois's parents didn't stop there. Since the rumors were apparently true and no guard made a surprise inspection, Lois's father went a step further. He invited the POWs inside the house.

Of course, they saved the best rule break for last.

"After dinner, Mom put slices of cake on six dinner plates, heaped them with strawberries and lots of whipped cream, and we took them to the prisoners," Lois remembers. "They all really enjoyed it and ate it every day they worked for us." It should come as little surprise, then, that they also ate dinner at the table with the family for the rest of their time on the farm, too.[1]

Many Americans would probably be astonished to learn that roughly 400,000 German, 51,000 Italian and 5,000 Japanese prisoners of war were held in the United States of America during World War II.[2] Their experiences have not been portrayed within popular culture as Allied POWs were in such films as 1963's *The Great Escape* or the 1960s sitcom *Hogan's Heroes*. Perhaps it's because there was a decided lack of drama. Escape attempts were rare (and those who did escape were usually rounded up within days), and sabotage operations on local factories and railroad tracks didn't exist. Not one act of sabotage by an escaped POW was ever reported.[3] The Axis POWs received exemplary treatment, so much so that they wrote to relatives in Germany begging them not to send any food but to keep it for themselves.

In short, sitting in an American POW camp wasn't a bad way to wait out the war. In fact, many POWs returned to the United States after the war and became American citizens. That's a claim no Allied POW in a German *stalag* or Japanese POW camp would ever make.

While the presence of prisoner of war camps in America garnered a lot of coverage from the press during the war, the swift appearance of the Korean War and the Cold War thrust the Axis POW experience into the back of many American minds. Many camps were located in fairly isolated areas and didn't remain in the national spotlight. In most cases, the physical evidence simply disappeared. After the POWs were sent home, the hastily erected camps were torn down or reconverted to their original purposes as fairgrounds or other facilities. Buildings were auctioned off to be used elsewhere, and records were lost.

Unfortunately, this has meant that research on specific topics—such as Nazism in the camps—has been harder to do. Many historians have decided to document this brief slice of American history by focusing on the camps at the state and regional level. Authors of the subject vary from professional historians to local, amateur historians. Thankfully, more scholarship continues to emerge. But time is running out to record the prisoners' and soldiers' personal stories.

Perhaps the best resource on this subject is Arnold Krammer's *Nazi Prisoners of War in America*. Antonio Thompson's more recent *Men in German Uniform* is also a worthy contribution. More and more scholarly and regional/local studies continue to appear, broadening our understanding of the camps and the prisoners themselves.

More work needs to be done on the Italian and Japanese POW experience in America, though there are some notable works already available. Recent studies include Ulrich Straus's *The Anguish of Surrender: Japanese POWs of World War II*, Louis E. Keefer's *Italian Prisoners of War in America: 1942–1946 Captives or Allies?* and the documentary *Prisoners in Paradise* by Camilla Calamandrei.

Nebraska POW Camps: A History of World War II Prisoners in the Heartland seeks to offer a general overview of the main camps in Nebraska during World War II and to show the excellent treatment they received at the hands of the United States. It also reveals how the United States decided to pursue a secret policy of reeducation for the German POWs in an attempt to eradicate their Nazi beliefs.

A note on the usage of POW vs. PW: During the war, the common term used was PW instead of POW. They will be used interchangeably here.

PART I
WELCOME TO AMERICA

CHAPTER 1

OVERVIEW OF THE U.S. POW CAMP SYSTEM

In June 1942, the number of prisoners of war held in Great Britain reached a critical juncture. Years of fighting Hitler had filled to capacity the camps housing Axis prisoners of war. British officials asked the U.S. State Department if it wouldn't mind taking some POWs off their hands—about fifty thousand of them. It took a few months to convince the Americans, but in the end, they eventually, albeit reluctantly, agreed.[4] Those fifty thousand POWs were only the beginning.

After months of haggling between U.S. government agencies to decide who would be in charge of the POW camp system in the United States, the Office of the Provost Marshal General (OPMG) finally organized the Prisoner of War Division under the direction of Assistant Provost General Brigadier General Blackshear M. Bryan.[5] In mid-September 1942, the OPMG submitted a proposal to the Joint Chiefs of Staff that outlined the program of camp construction for the first fifty thousand prisoners arriving from the British camps. Since immediate action was required, they decided their best option would be to use abandoned Civilian Conservation Corps camps built during the Depression. They also considered using fairgrounds, unused sections of military bases, auditoriums and even tent cities.

The Civilian Conservation Corps camps were perfect for housing POWs, as they had been built as barracks near rural work projects, they were empty and available and they were located mainly in the South and Southwest, far removed from the war industries of the Midwest and the Eastern seaboard. Placing other camps in less populated areas of the country commanded by the Fourth, Seventh and Eighth Service Commands also offered a logical solution for minimizing the fear of prisoners escaping to highly populated areas, like New York City and Washington, D.C. Eighteen states composed this region, including Nebraska, which was under the Seventh Service Command.[6]

POW camps were classified as Class I installations and put under the jurisdiction of the commanding general of the camp area's Service Command. Sometimes this created problems since it put the OPMG out of direct control of the camps themselves, making camp administration even more difficult. As many camps were located on military posts, the camp commander of the prisoners was directly responsible to the military post commander, who in turn was responsible to the service command.[7]

When the public found out about the POW camps, they were naturally alarmed. They worried about escapes, sabotage and "potential personal danger."[8] Because of security reasons, the location and construction of the camps remained a top priority. The War Department ordered that the sites were to be isolated and away from "black-out" areas, which extended 150 miles in from the Mexican and Canadian borders, 75 miles inland from both coasts and nowhere near shipyards or vital war industries.[9]

The War Department drew up a basic plan for the construction and layout that all new camps throughout the United States would follow. Each camp administration would then look over the plans and propose any necessary changes specific to its campsite. All camps had to follow the guidelines set forth in the Geneva Convention of 1929. Major Maxwell S. McKnight of the OPMG's office outlined the camp layout as follows:

The basic feature of the plan is the compound. A camp consists of one or more compounds surrounded by two wire fences. Compounds are separated from each other by a single fence. Each compound houses four companies or prisoners or approximately 1,000 prisoners. The housing and messing facilities are equivalent to those furnished to United States troops at base camps as required by the Geneva Convention. These facilities consist of five barracks, a latrine containing showers and laundry tubs with unlimited hot and cold running water, a mess hall, and an administrative building for each company. In addition, each compound is provided with a recreation building, an infirmary, a workshop, a canteen building, and an administration building. The compound area is sufficient to provide outdoor recreation space. Each camp also has a chapel, a station hospital, and a large outdoor recreation area for the use of all prisoners at the camp. At some camps located on an Army post, certain wards of the post hospital are designated for the use of prisoners of war in lieu of a station hospital at the prisoner of war camp.[10]

For the administration part of the camp, there was a central guardhouse, a main administration building and a tool house combined with an office. There were also "quartermaster offices, warehouses (including cold storage), shops, fire house, and other miscellaneous facilities specific to a particular project."[11] Camps usually included a post office, warehouse and utility area. Some camps, like Fort Robinson, also included a bakery, post exchange, library and movie theater.[12] This layout was essentially the same for all camps throughout the United States. Building anything more substantial would have cost the army more time and money.

Typical of the stoves used in all POW camps. This one was in Camp Atlanta and is now on display at the local museum. *Nebraska Prairie Museum.*

23

Officers and enlisted men were usually not in the same camp, or if they were, they were segregated in separate commands and separate barracks. American guard personnel came from military escort companies (MPs). With the influx of POWs, the OPMG requested that more MP companies be activated so that there would be approximately three prisoners to each guard. Of course, this figure differed depending on how many prisoners were at each camp. Security also differed. Some camps used watchtowers or watchdogs while others used "four-man patrols within the compound."[13]

People in communities near the camps watched the construction with a mixture of curiosity and fear. Who, exactly, were these prisoners? Were they really the menacing Nazis seen in Hollywood movies and on propaganda posters? They were about to find out.

THE "GERMAN" POWS

The Axis POWs came to America in three distinct waves. The first group came in 1943 from North Africa and southern Italy. This group included Italians and Germans, ardent Nazis, members of the Kriegsmarine and Erwin Rommel's infamous *Afrika Korps*. The second wave came from northern France after the D-Day invasion of June 6, 1944, and included less elite soldiers. POWs captured from the winter of 1944 through Germany's defeat in May 1945 constituted the third wave and consisted of the remnants of Hitler's once grand *Wehrmacht*.

It is important to note, though, that of the German POWs, not all were true Germans. Instead, the German military machine consisted of men from Germany's allies; western, northern and Eastern European nations; forced conscription; and even prisoners and concentration camp inmates from the Reich. Countries represented in the German army included countries from all of Europe and the Soviet Union. This clash of cultures and ideals naturally created a problem for the German military, but when those men became prisoners of war, those problems took on a whole new significance within the camps. As historian Antonio Thompson notes, the Americans didn't take these fundamental dissimilarities into consideration.

Little thought was given to the differences between the men in German uniform. Besides, what would it matter if Fritz or Hans came from Austria or Poland or was a Democratic Socialist or National Socialist? They were still German, still the enemy, and all Nazis. Aryan mythology aside, the prisoners came from across Europe and Asia. Brown-skinned and brown-eyed soldiers of every conceivable age mingled with the "Teutonic" blond-haired, blue-eyed "German" youth. Germans and non-Germans and Nazis and non-Nazis mixed with the ideologically unsuitable, socially undesirable, and physically and emotionally unreliable. Some of these warriors used to feed the Nazi war machine had little or no grasp of the German language. While the Americans considered the German soldiers a homogenous group, the men in German uniform always remained conscious of the distinction.[14]

The average American, of course, made no distinction between German or Austrian or Pole. Neither did they distinguish between "Nazi" and "German." To them, they were one and the same. This was also true of contemporary media. More often than not, in newspaper and magazine stories, radio shows and newsreels, Germans were referred to as Nazis en masse, as though the two words were completely interchangeable. Indeed, this phenomenon is still alive and well today.

But one could be an Axis soldier and not subscribe to Nazi ideology. The impact of these competing worldviews and the failure of the Americans to properly screen prisoners for ideological purposes would combine to create a hotly contested battle for control of the camps between the Nazis and the anti-Nazis. It also led to the birth of the U.S. Army's top secret Intellectual Diversion Program, i.e. "reeducation."

Many of these non-German POWs wanted to be transferred away from the more radical Nazi elements. The archives for Camp Atlanta, Camp Scottsbluff and Fort Robinson are full of transfer requests from these men. These requests were from Czechs, French, Polish and numerous others. A group of thirty Yugoslavian POWs wrote a letter to the Yugoslav Legation in Washington, D.C., for help in returning to Yugoslavia in April 1945.

One prisoner at Camp Scottsbluff, Cedric Goedecke, was a German who had lived and worked with his family running a coffee and tea import and foodstuffs business in Switzerland since 1926. He served as an interpreter with the Fifth Panzer Armee Kommando headquarters in Tunis and was taken prisoner at Poto-Farina in May 1943. He wrote a letter to "competent authorities" in Omaha and Washington, D.C., in which he documented how he had come to serve in the German Army.

I was drafted into the Army through the German Consulate in Switzerland on 14 July 1942. I was informed that if I would not comply I would have to suffer the consequences. Switzerland at that time was surrounded by the German Armies. An occupation of Switzerland on account of any war developments was then within the realm of possibilities. The fear that I would bring disaster to my entire family caused me to comply with the German authorities...I have never belonged to the National Socialist Party, to the Labor Front or any organization connected with the NSDAP...I am urgently needed in my business...I beg you to examine my request and to permit, if at all possible, my return to my family in Switzerland at the earliest possible moment, and if at all possible without having to be sent to Germany at first.[15]

After obtaining permission from the Swiss government through the International Red Cross, Captain Duell, the assistant director of security and intelligence at Camp Scottsbluff, gave his stamp of approval for Cedric's transfer, stating that Goedecke was "completely reliable and trustworthy." General Somervell gave his permission on October 26, 1945.[16]

THE AXIS POWS ARRIVE

POWs were processed at the point of capture: "Ideally, POW screening involved completing the basic personnel record with the soldier's name, serial number, and fingerprints; a list of items in his possession; and other identifying characteristics."[17] Of course, this didn't always go as planned, what with the chaotic scene at the front lines.

The POWs were transported via empty troop and supply ships that were returning to America from the war zone. They arrived at Camp Shanks, New York, or Norfolk, Virginia. Here, the U.S. Army managed those POWs who hadn't yet undergone processing. From the East Coast, prisoners usually boarded trains to their destination. Many POWs expressed shock and awe at the incredible expanse of land they crossed, not to mention the fact that the cities were still standing, having "miraculously" escaped the numerous Luftwaffe raids reported by Hitler's propaganda machine. One German POW, Dietrich Kohl, decided to make a list of each town his train went through in case he wanted to escape. The list was quite long, starting in Newport News, Virginia, and ending with "Chadron, Whitney, Crawford." Once he arrived at Fort Robinson, he never did try to escape.[18]

Another round of processing awaited POWs once they arrived at their POW camp. According to the Guard Regulations handbook at Fort

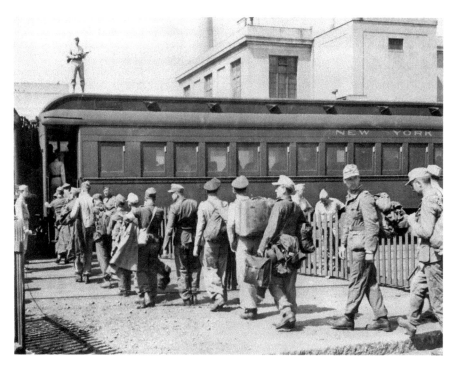

After their trip across the Atlantic, POWs board a train in Boston bound for the camps. *Wikimedia Commons, National Archives.*

Robinson, all prisoners were given a physical examination and searched under an officer's supervision. Unauthorized articles such as "weapons, money, signal devices, (cameras, flash lights, binoculars, codes or cyphers and radio transmitters), and papers or books containing pictures or maps of military or naval installations" were confiscated and taken into the custody of camp authorities. Strangely enough, at Fort Robinson, a Chihuahua dog was found in a prisoner's overcoat pocket.[19]

If the prisoners arrived at night, they were served "sandwiches and hot coffee." Each prisoner was issued "one pillow, two blankets, one bedsack or mattress, and straw for the sack when issued, and one metal or canvas cot."[20]After their arrival, the German Red Cross informed the POWs' families of their whereabouts.

Despite being behind barbed wire, the POWs continued to function within an organized structure. They chose a spokesperson from their ranks who served as their representative to the government authorities. This allowed the POWs to communicate with representatives of the State and

War Departments, camp commanders, members of the Swiss delegation (the neutral protecting power), the YMCA, the International Red Cross (IRC) and the Lutheran Commission. Officers and enlisted men also had a spokesman and enjoyed orderlies and cooks from POW ranks. All in all, the system within the compound was quite orderly. But this self-sufficiency fostered an atmosphere of continued militarism and promoted the same political ideology found throughout the German military. It would cause immense problems in the future.[21]

DAILY LIFE AT A PRISONER OF WAR CAMP

The Geneva Convention of 1929 controlled all regulations of camp life. This included food rations, clothing allowances, sending and receiving mail, health and medical care, religion, education, recreation and labor. The U.S. Army sought to follow the convention to the letter. Ignoring it put American POWs in Germany and elsewhere at risk. To make certain the rules were followed, a representative of the IRC made periodic inspections with a representative of the Special War Projects Division of the State Department accompanying them. The War Prisoner's Aid, part of the World's Committee of the YMCA based in Geneva, Switzerland, also sent representatives.[22]

One of those YMCA representatives was Howard Hong. In May 1943, the St. Olaf College professor attended a lecture given by John R. Mott, the head of the World Alliance of the YMCA, about giving aid to interred POWs. Hong was moved by the speech and asked Mott if he could work for the YMCA. As a result, Hong became one of the first employed for POW fieldwork.

According to Minnesota historian Dean B. Simmons, Hong had two reasons for working with the program:

> [H]e viewed the work of War Prisoners Aid as a respectable and inviting alternative to active military involvement in the war. Moreover, he had been working on Kierkegaard's Works of Love, which has been described as "one of the most elegant descriptions of what the imitation of Jesus—the life of Christian love—should be." The YMCA's work with prisoners, as Hong saw it, had all the essential qualities of such a life.

Fifty years later, Hong told Simmons, "I never worked so hard in my life. I like to work, but it was there to do, and there was good reason to do it. But that reason was not political, it was not a matter of law, it was a matter of the universally human, you see."[23]

Though schedules varied at each camp, the prisoners at Fort Robinson began their day at 6:00 a.m. with roll call at 6:30 a.m. Breakfast was served at 6:45 a.m., dinner at noon and supper at 5:30 p.m. Barracks inspection occurred every morning at 10:00 a.m. The prisoners were only allowed thirty minutes to eat their meals, and "wasting food will not be tolerated." Showers and shaves were required twice a week, and bedding was aired Friday morning of every week. Prisoners had recreation facilities available, as well as church services on Sunday morning.

Of course, one of the most important rules concerned where a prisoner of war should *not* be: beyond the barbed wire fence. "Anyone doing so," the Guard Regulations handbook said, "will be warned by the sentry in the tower and failure to heed such warning will result in serious consequences."[24] Regulations were established for visitors ("received between the hours of 1:00 p.m. and 4:30 p.m."), inspections and sanitation.[25]

Perhaps the best source of information on the prisoners' daily life comes from the aforementioned inspection reports. Each report lists different categories, including religion, music, education, theater, arts and crafts, athletics and books. It's not hard to see that the United States took great pains to follow the Geneva Convention as well as to offer a wide variety of activities for the prisoners. The old quote "idle hands are the devil's playground" also applied here. When keeping their minds and bodies occupied, prisoners had far less opportunity to create mischief. But remarkably, not many men *wanted* to create mischief. They knew how good they had it in America, especially considering that many of their comrades were starving to death in Soviet gulags.

The Axis POWs had all the comforts of home. Each camp had a canteen where they could "purchase sweets, crackers, fresh fruit, soft drinks, and such other food products and supplies as approved by the camp commander."[26] The profits from canteen sales went toward purchasing "sports and recreational articles, furniture and draperies for day rooms, theatrical and musical supplies, books for the camp library, and the like." Clothing, especially specific items needed for outdoor labor such as gloves, goggles and hard-toed shoes, was furnished. Outer clothing was stamped with "PW" in bold letters.[27]

All prisoners enjoyed freedom of religion and could go to services held in the camps. Educational projects, such as classes in English and other courses, were permitted and encouraged, and prisoners had access to books and periodicals from around the country—providing they met with the censors' approval.

A canteen coupon from Camp Atlanta. They came in cent denominations of one, five, ten and twenty-five. *Photo courtesy Dave Frank.*

Prisoners were also given sports equipment for both outdoor and indoor games as well as handicraft tools and supplies to put on theatrical productions.

In short, no prisoner of war lacked for food, clothing or recreational activities. The same could undoubtedly not be said for the German army.

CONTROVERSIES

Perhaps contrary to what their propaganda had warned them to expect, German and Italian POWs were treated remarkably well, especially compared to their American counterparts. But as the war went on and the public became more aware of their living conditions, grumbling and outright condemnation over how good the enemy had it began to appear. Camps earned the nickname "the Fritz Ritz."[28] Articles abounded in popular magazines. *Collier's* ran a story on October 14, 1944, with the headline, "Our 'Pampered War Prisoners'" and then proceeded to share why the Germans and Italians were most certainly *not* coddled but rather treated fairly under Geneva Convention regulations. The author of the article, Robert Devore, stated that he had probably seen more POWs than anyone else, save for government and Red Cross organizations, and said, "I saw no tender treatment. I heard an American commander tell a

German labor detail it could do an honest day's work or loaf indefinitely on bread and water. At the same camp, Japanese prisoners marched back to work one morning before the bayonets of American soldiers."[29] *LIFE* magazine even reported in November 1944 that charges of the U.S. coddling the POWs had led to a congressional investigation of the matter. "According to unofficial reports, [the committee] has decided that charges of coddling are unwarranted."[30]

Perhaps the charges were unwarranted, but it didn't stop some American citizens from expressing their frustration. Former German POW William Oberdieck was held in Camp Atlanta, arriving in January 1944. Years later, he still remembered the woman who came up to the fence. "One evening there was a woman, I will never forget, who began screaming, 'Here they sit, and over there they shoot up our boys!'" Oberdieck recalled. "She got so upset, they called the captain, and they accompanied her home."[31]

Another area of contention was the caliber of the U.S. enlisted men who worked in the POW camps. The U.S. soldiers who were transferred to POW camps were altogether different than those who were at the front lines in Europe and Asia. The majority of the personnel was made up of those who were found "unsatisfactory" for combat, "physically and psychologically unfit, recently retired officers...combat veterans recycled home; and raw recruits." Major Maxwell McKnight of the OPMG stated in 1942, "We were pretty much dredging the bottom of the barrel. We had all kinds of kooks and wacky people."[32] Of course, the caliber of guards differed from camp to camp, but as historian Arnold Krammer points out, even the official historian of the Army Services Forces, John Millett, said that the POW camps "tended to be a dumping ground...for field grade officers who were found to be unsatisfactory."[33]

After being injured in service, Steve Sorok was assigned to work as a mail carrier at the Scottsbluff POW Camp. "The signature of the camp was Service Command Unit 4752," he remembered, "but we always ridiculed it as 'Sick, Crippled, and Useless' because most of these [American] men were either of limited service or limited assignment."[34]

"Unsatisfactory" U.S. soldiers brought about a host of problems, but one of the biggest was how they treated the prisoners. Some men, after being in combat, simply hated the Germans. Others were disgruntled with being assigned to a POW camp instead of in the thick of fighting. A field service camp survey taken at Camp Scottsbluff in February 1945 asked, "What is the general attitude of the guard personnel towards prisoners of war?" Scrawled in pencil beneath it are the words, "Bunch of Krauts and bastards."[35] According to a Special Projects report from the OPMG, there was no doubt as to the caliber of the American guards: "The quality of this personnel is, as in other camps, very low. Fifteen or twenty of them are psycho-neurotics."[36]

Again, the nation took notice. An article appeared in the *Boston Globe* that revealed the overwhelming incompetence of the U.S. guards, from their poor treatment of the POWs to their complete inefficiency. The War Department immediately launched into training mode, creating a three-week training program and a reference manual on the proper treatment of POWs.[37] Thereafter, conditions improved.

Escapes

When some prisoners saw just how big the United States of America was, they put aside all plans to try and escape. Others refused to be deterred. Though there were some successful escapes from Nebraska camps, all POWs were captured or returned on their own free will. One rather amazing escape was found buried in the records of Camp Scottsbluff. Somehow, Sergeant Wolfgang Kurzer and Corporal Karl Tomola escaped Camp Scottsbluff and made it all the way to Philadelphia, Pennsylvania, before they were apprehended and held at Fort Meade in Maryland. Kurzer ended up being transferred to Camp Huntsville in Texas, while Tomola ostensibly stayed in Fort Meade for the duration of the war.[38]

Overall, escapes were not a big issue within the camps. Krammer's studies confirm this. "Escapes, in fact, occurred infrequently, most large camps experiencing no more than three or four such events during the entire war."[39]

Labor

Long before the first POWs came to the United States, the country was already experiencing a labor shortage—and it was only getting worse. Migrant workers, women and high school students were helping as much as they could, but even they weren't filling the demand. With thousands of able-bodied prisoners soon to become available, the answer became clear: the POWs could be used as a labor source.

However, the Geneva Convention strictly regulated the kinds of labor prisoners could undertake, and it also raised confusing issues. The War Department set up the Prisoner of War Employment Reviewing Board to try to iron out the guidelines for prisoner labor. The board finally decided that the work could not be directly related to any war operations and could not be "unhealthful, dangerous, degrading, or beyond the particular prisoner's physical capacity."[40] This left the door wide open for a variety of tasks, and the government wasted no time in utilizing its new manpower.[41]

At its most basic, there were two classes of labor: paid and unpaid. Unpaid labor consisted of work that benefited the prisoners

An Italian POW poses with his work gloves at Camp Scottsbluff. *Legacy of the Plains Museum.*

themselves, i.e. work that took place in camp. This included working in the administrative offices, camp maintenance, working at the canteen or in the kitchen or even being a tailor or barber. Paid labor was anything that did not fall into this category. POWs could not do any type of work that dealt with war operations. Article 31 of the Geneva Convention was very specific about this. "It is especially prohibited to use prisoners for the manufacture and transportation of arms or munitions of any kind, or for transporting material intended for combatant units."[42]

Officer prisoners were not required to work, and noncommissioned officers could do supervisory work. However, the German High Command "officially informed the German prisoners in the United States that it considers performance of work by non-commissioned officers and officers in the prisoners' own interest as it furthers the maintenance of their physical

ealth." Payment was set at eighty cents a day and was paid in
)ons. Working hours were the same as civilians doing the same
ιγμ . . in the area.[43]

By early 1943, POWs were being sent to military installations first and
foremost to help relieve men who were needed for overseas duty. However,
it wasn't until the fall of 1943 that the government had hammered out the
regulations necessary to allow the POWs into the civilian workforce where
they were badly needed, especially in the agricultural sector.

Known as "contract labor," business leaders in nearby communities and
chambers of commerce could petition the War Department for their labor
needs.[44] These potential employers had to jump through numerous hoops
to get POW labor, but as Arnold Krammer points out, "It should be noted
that as exasperating as these regulations and delays may have been to the
labor-starved employer, the government's central concern was, as always, the
welfare of the POWs, and through them, the safety of the American POWs
in German hands."[45]

Large base camps would not be sufficient for housing the more than
100,000 prisoners who would be working in private industry in locations
away from the base camp. Thus, the War Department created a network
of branch camps. The POWs would be working in industries such as
logging, meatpacking, mining, railroads, foundry work and agriculture. But
transporting men back and forth between the camp and their jobs had to
be minimized. This meant that these branch camps varied in how many
prisoners they could hold and what the layouts looked like. Some of these
camps were "tent cities" or were in places like the county fairgrounds.
More than five hundred such camps were built across the country with the
capability to hold around 250 to 750 prisoners in each. The branch camps
were made available expressly for this purpose.

By May 1945, 141 permanent camps and 319 branch camps existed. New
prisoners, upon their initial arrival, were subsequently tested for particular
skills. This was then recorded in their personnel records. In this way, when
particular needs arose for the military or for the local agricultural industry,
for example, POWs could be directly transferred to branch camps for these
temporary jobs.[46]

As we shall see through studying the labor program at the Nebraska camps,
utilizing POW labor became crucial to keeping the state's economy moving.

CHAPTER 2

NAZISM AND REEDUCATION IN THE POW CAMPS

In the quiet rolling hills and buttes of the Fort Robinson camp, far away from the battles raging on European soil, Nazism was alive and well. Prisoner of war *Stabsfeldwebel* Harry Huenmoerder, a thirty-seven-year-old senior-ranking noncommissioned officer from Hamburg, was pro-Nazi. Worse, he'd been elected camp spokesman. Huenmoerder had been in the German military for over thirteen years, and Hitler's rhetoric had taken root. He came to Fort Robinson in November 1943 with the first batch of prisoners captured in Tunisia by the British. According to a Field Service Camp Survey of February 15, 1945, his character was "beyond reproach. He is honest and sincere in his dealings, commands the respect of the Commanding Officer as well as the men of the compound."[47]

Huenmoerder's pro-Nazi tendencies were no secret to the other prisoners. Indeed, they had elected him to his post. Unfortunately, camps with Nazi spokesmen were not uncommon and became "models of efficiency." A well-run camp would endear the Nazis to the American command. This apparently became evident to those with anti-Nazis feelings. Historian Tom Buecker suggests that "the Americans seemed to have an unwritten policy of making any concession which helped keep the compounds running smoothly…The general aim of the American command was to maintain tranquility."[48]

Many incidents involving Nazism occurred at camps throughout the United States, including those in Nebraska. At Fort Robinson, prisoner Ernst Guenther Ummack was put into protective custody because his life had been threatened by other POWs for reading and translating American newspapers.[49] Gefreiter Otto Ludwig had made anti-Nazi statements in the camp, one of which Spokesman Huenmoerder recorded in a letter attached to the transfer order. "Inquires [sic] made with the Company leader Co.A., reported that LUDWIG at dinnertime used in the Mess hall Co. A. the following sentence, directed to his comrades, "If we win the war, I will never return to Germany, if we loose [sic] it I will 'deliver the Nazis to the knife.'" Ludwig was put in protective custody to "prevent harm from befalling him at the hands of the other prisoners" and was transferred to Camp McCain, Mississippi, a mere four days after the incident was reported.[50]

Despite transfers, Nazism in the camps continued to worsen. Eventually, weeding out Nazis from the anti-Nazis became the tool of choice to control the violence. On July 17, 1944, a comprehensive directive from the War Department sought to solve the problem by segregating the Nazis from the anti-Nazis. All German army officer prisoners were to be separated from their noncommissioned officers and enlisted men and put into either the anti-Nazi camp at Camp Ruston, Louisiana, or into the pro-Nazi camp at Camp Alva, Oklahoma. German NCOs were isolated at camps designated for their service command. For the Seventh Service Command, in which all Nebraska camps fell, they were to be transferred to Camp Clark, Missouri.[51]

Alfred Thompson, intelligence officer and assistant executive officer of Fort Robinson, wrote a letter on March 5, 1946, detailing another incident involving a prisoner named Tillman Oeckerath, who suffered from a double hernia. According to Thompson, he "worked hard" at Fort Robinson and left with a good recommendation. Because of his ailment, his physical records advised he be given only light labor. But as soon as Oeckerath was transferred to Camp Scottsbluff, the pro-Nazis who had been with him at Fort Robinson and were now in Scottsbluff immediately remembered his anti-Nazi sentiments. As punishment for such views, Oeckerath was thrown into the guardhouse because he could not work in the beet fields with the rest of the POWs.[52]

According to Thompson, the hospital at Scottsbluff "reeked with Nazi influence." He claimed the doctors were all *Parteigenossen*, or party members, and the clerks and assistants were "equally as politically rotten":

When a man reported to the infirmary on sick call, he was questioned by the Nazi non-com, probed as to his political opinion, and if found politically favorable, was admitted to the hospital for an examination. If he were hospitalized, he found the system controlled from top to bottom with political criminals. At early morning he was awakened by the sound of hob-nailed boots of the Nazi non-com. He ate breakfast under prescribed rules of etiquette and tribute to the Nazi doctors. When the officer doctors arrived in the ward he drew himself to attention whether he was incapable of standing, or if he could stand; all this happened after the defeat of the third reich [sic].[53]

Nazism had come to Nebraska. But what could be done about it?

THE INTELLECTUAL DIVERSION PROGRAM

As early as March 1943, the War Department recognized the need to break the grip of Nazism in the POW camps through reeducation. According to the proposal sent to General Frederick Osborn of the Information and Education Division through General George C. Marshall, the program's goal would be such that "prisoners of war might be exposed to the facts of American history, the workings of a democracy and the contributions made to America by peoples of all national origins."[54]

Yet Major General Allen W. Gullion, provost marshal general at the time, thought the plan unwise: "Enemy prisoners of war are, for the most part, not children. Those who have sufficient intellectual capacity to be of value to a post-war world have already built the philosophical frameworks of their respective lives. Those whose minds are sufficiently plastic to be affected by the program are probably not worth the effort."[55] The plan was shelved on June 24, 1943.

Unfortunately, stories continued to emerge on the Nazi-related violence in the camps. The public became frustrated at the lack of government action, and the situation soon became fodder for editorials, columnists and letters to the editors. Even Eleanor Roosevelt became involved after Dorothy Bromley of the *New York Herald Tribune* and syndicated columnist Dorothy Thompson presented the problem to her. Mrs. Roosevelt spoke to her husband, who then spoke to the Secretaries of War and State. They in turn told the new provost marshal general, Archer L. Lerch, to get out the year-old plan produced by General Marshall.[56]

However, despite the public outcry and demand for resolution of the Nazism problem, the War Department knew it faced several important obstacles. The most important concerned the Geneva Convention's rule

The front of this German propaganda leaflet shows how "well" POWs were treated by the Germans. They would drop these over Allied troop locations. *Ed Reep Collection. Courtesy of Susan Reep.*

prohibiting enemies from being subject to propaganda. This carried far-reaching overtones. If word leaked of German prisoners being "reeducated," American POWs held in Germany might then be subject to retaliation. Therefore, the need to keep the program a secret stemmed from the government's desire to protect American POWs.[57]

But how to get past the Geneva Convention's rule? Thankfully, Article 17 contained the necessary loophole. The article stated, "So far as possible, belligerents shall encourage intellectual diversions and sports organized by prisoners of war." Since intellectual diversion was advocated, it remained up to the War Department to pick and choose the proper subjects and media. The representatives of the War Department and the State Department determined "that if selected media for intellectual diversion were made available in the camps, the curiosity of the prisoners concerning the United States and its institutions would provide the means for their reeducation."[58]

Remarkably, even before the advent of the Intellectual Diversion Program in late 1944, POWs had already flocked to the classroom largely by their own initiative. Arnold Krammer noted, "The question of classroom facilities was

PRISONERS-OF-WAR GET A SQUARE DEAL

GERMANY STRICTLY OBSERVES
GENEVA CONVENTION

Prisoners-of-war tell us they expected to be shot or ill-treated by the Germans as their officers had warned them they would.

> *These POW don't look as if they were shot dead, ill-treated, starved or beaten-up, do they?*

They are enjoying cigarettes just received from the Red Cross. Through the International Red Cross every POW gets one parcel a week containing cigarettes, chocolate, biscuits and other useful and pleasant things. Note the solidly constructed barracks in the rear.

No. 2 *of a series of twelve leaflets showing the life of prisoners-of-war in German camps.*

AI-117-10-44

The backside of this German propaganda leaflet emphasizes that the Germans followed the Geneva Convention regulations for POWs. *Ed Reep Collection. Courtesy of Susan Reep.*

first raised by the inmates themselves almost immediately after arriving in camp." Education became so popular that the Reich Ministry of Education set up a program to offer credits for college and high school in May 1944. Fifteen major German and Austrian universities would accept the grades at "face value" and make it possible for the prisoners to actually earn their degrees while in America. If the degree they wanted wasn't offered through those universities, the OPMG made it possible for them to take extension courses at nearby colleges or universities. During the POWs' duration in America, they studied from 103 different universities and technical colleges in America.[59]

But those courses were about to get an injection of American democracy. The Intellectual Diversion program was put under the command of the OPMG. It in turn created a subcommittee to establish the program's policy and procedures. The program officially started on September 6, 1944. However, the American public still remained unaware of the secret program and continued to disparage the War Department. An article appeared in the *Atlantic Monthly* entitled "What to Do with German Prisoners," which criticized the "stupidity" of the government in handling the POWs. By the time this article appeared in November, personnel had already started to arrive at the camps in order to begin the reeducation program.[60]

Under the direction of Colonel Edward Davison and Major Maxwell McKnight, the Prisoners of War Special Projects Division was formed with a variety of academics and intellectuals. This staff worked at 50 Broadway in New York City:[61]

> *The core objective of the plan was outlined by the Provost Marshal General's Office. The prisoners would be given facts, objectively presented but so selected and assembled as to correct misinformation and prejudices surviving Nazi conditioning. The facts, rather than being forced upon them, would be made available through such medias [sic] as literature, motion pictures, newspapers, music, art, and educational courses. Two types of facts were needed: those which would convince them of the impracticality and viciousness of the Nazi position. If a large variety of facts could be presented convincingly, perhaps the German prisoners of war might understand and believe historical and ethical truth as generally conceived by Western civilization, might come to respect the American people and their ideological values, and upon repatriation to Germany might form the nucleus of a new German ideology which will reject militarism and totalitarian controls and will advocate a democratic system of government.[62]*

To fulfill such a lofty goal, the Idea Factory, as it came to be known, was born. Located at Fort Kearny, Rhode Island, the Idea Factory consisted of German POWs who were carefully screened for their anti-Nazi tendencies and then selected after they filled out questionnaires. These prisoners were then separated from the rest of their comrades at their camp to await transport to Fort Kearny. Although this selection was not foolproof, the Americans did have an advantage. Hitler's impending defeat had soured many Germans against Nazism. Others had never been ardent admirers of Nazism. Still, at the time the reeducation program appeared, many of the German POWs had been prisoners for two or three years, offering them ample opportunity to think about Germany's status in the world.[63] These prisoners were involved in the experimental phase of the reeducation program. Although pro-Nazism was still a problem in the camps, this group was determined to do something about it.

The Special Projects staff then assembled a division of "specially-qualified" German prisoners—writers, professors and linguists who were dedicated anti-Nazis. All were volunteers, all were officers and all renounced their *Wehrmacht* ranks. Due to this special assignment, these prisoners enjoyed far more freedom at Fort Kearny than they had had at their respective camps. No guards or towers policed their movements, and they even took the ferry to Jamestown in army trucks to pick up their supplies.[64]

However, this rather elite group of individuals was perhaps not the most prudent choice. Although the group was happy to be among other intellectuals, Ron Robin believed the group did not understand the tastes of the average prisoner. According to Robin, this would come to negatively affect the program.

The Idea Factory was separated into subdivisions, which included review sections for film and government agency material, translation sections for the school curriculum and a camp newspaper section. This last section monitored around seventy POW camp newspapers as well as produced its own nationwide camp newspaper called *Der Ruf (The Call).*[65] The goals of the newspaper were to "reflect the experience of being a German PW in America, but also stimulate democratic thinking." The first issue appeared in the spring of 1945.

When Germany fell and victory was proclaimed in Europe in May 1945, many of the ordinary classes POWs had been taking were eliminated. Instead, the essentials—English, history, geography and others that stressed democracy—were emphasized. Now the men at the Idea Factory in New York concentrated on reviewing and preparing materials for the new reeducation

41

program. They focused on two areas: censorship and translations. Books that were to be considered for class use, libraries and for sale in the POW canteen all had to be read, analyzed and evaluated before they would be declared "suitable" for the POWs.[66]

This would prove to be more difficult than originally anticipated. The War Prisoners' Aid Committee of the International YMCA and the International Red Cross had sent books published in Germany to the camps. The German government had also provided them with *Soldatenbriefe*, elementary textbooks prepared especially for the German Armed Forces. Upon close inspection of the camp libraries, officials discovered that the majority of material contained some Nazi propaganda. To eliminate this problem, the Special Projects Division first censored all available books in the camps. Commanding officers then compiled a list of book titles from their libraries and sent the lists to the Factory's Review Section. Those books coming directly from Germany were examined before being shipped to the camps. In June 1945, a list had been compiled of those books, both approved and disapproved, and was then distributed to the assistant executive officers and intelligence officers of the camps.[67]

With so many diversions already in place before the reeducation program went into effect, it remained imperative that the Special War Projects Division find U.S. officers capable of implementing the program. The requirements were stiff. The men were expected to be experts on German and American journalism, film and literature; be fluent in German; and have previous experience in a POW camp and education. These assistant executive officers were trained at conferences in Fort Slocum, New York, in late 1944 and early 1945.[68]

The importance of intelligence officers to the program's success could not be overstated. Yet more often than not, they met with more opposition from their own officers and American servicemen than from the prisoners themselves. Alfred Thompson suggests that the program did not receive the support and cooperation it should have at the camp level because of the intense secrecy surrounding it. Because it was a top secret program, they could not even tell their fellow officers just what they were doing. "One went so far as to tell his commanding officers that he was under secret orders and could not reveal his mission even to him. Some of the AEO's had enough brains to recognize the difficulties which would be involved in such complete secrecy and lack of confidence in co-workers, but the majority was not so intelligent." In fact, Thompson and other officers found themselves ostracized by their own co-workers. "We were called 'Junior Dick Tracys' or 'Super Sleuths' to the point where it hurt."[69]

This attitude originated from the very top. The supervising officer of the assistant executive officers, Major Paul A. Neuland, felt that the lack of contact between the officers in the field and the Special Projects Division chain of command was having a detrimental effect on the program itself. Even though he tried to pass along the critical comments of the officers to division headquarters, he succeeded only in alienating himself further from his fellow officers. Neuland was upset by the continual rejection of the officers' comments "by a man in the New York Office...doesn't make sense." But unfortunately, to his fellow Special War Projects Division officers, Neuland's criticism only pointed to a lack of loyalty.[70]

Thompson's letters echo Neuland's sentiments, though he described the problem somewhat more colorfully. After the war, Thompson was sent to Fort Eustis, Virginia, along with many other assistant executive officers to participate at the School for Democracy, where prisoners with anti-Nazi credentials underwent intensive democracy training courses. A member of the staff from Washington asked Thompson and other officers what they felt the success of the program was, to criticize it "without fear of reprisal." Thompson delivered the following tirade:

> *Why we were not asked when we could have helped, when we were in direct contact with the PW in the field, when we could have given suggestions which might have spelled the victory so badly needed on this front. But, we were distrusted from above, thought to be incapable of criticizing, incapable of thinking as adult manhood; we who were in direct contact with the problem, who were interested in the work and who gave everything to try to put it across were subordinated and silenced before a bunch of blabbering idols and idiots who knew nothing other than to polish their own brass and the brass of the next highest man.*[71]

These intelligence officers' responsibility carried further than merely implementing the reeducation program. They were also required to keep morale and special service activities "maintained and improved" for the American military personnel at the camps. They were ordered to distribute the War Department pamphlets 19-1 "What about the German Prisoners?" and 19-2 "Facts vs. Fantasy" to help in this endeavor.[72] Yet with the majority of the responsibility of the program falling on their shoulders, it is difficult to understand why the commanders in the Special Projects Division office did not listen more to their thoughts on the matter.

Yet the very nature of those in charge, who were mostly from academia, might offer a clue. As Ron Robin states in *The Barbed-Wire College*, "They represented an alienated intelligentsia, who never bothered to hide their contempt for the rank and file within the camps."[73] Robin's concept is worth consideration. While the intentions and ideas of the hierarchy of the Special Projects Division might have been quite noble, when it came to actually implementing the ideas, the intelligence officers and others involved encountered roadblocks. For example, the elevated language used in *Der Ruf* prevented it from being a success. This same mentality also carried over into other areas of the program.

Thompson's letters offer another clue. By late 1945, the Intellectual Diversion Program was in full swing. New equipment, such as projectors, phonographs, maps, charts, duplicating machines and typewriters had been added to the classroom. Prisoner enthusiasm for the classes was high. Yet after Germany's defeat, the OPMG office shifted gears. Thompson was beyond frustrated. "One could say, therefore, that the PMG had its eye set upon a goal and was on the road to success—until they threw a bucket of cold water over the entire setup when they became too excited and too hurried in their search for perfection."

Thompson believed the OPMG jeopardized the success of the program since it "ordered all courses other than courses of an indoctrinary nature to be dropped. This meant all courses in the sciences, music, art, engineering and languages other than English were to be immediately discontinued without explanation for their discontinuance given." Since the war had come to an end, the OPMG wished to cram as much "democratic" material as possible into the prisoners' minds.

But Thompson saw a disturbing development at Fort Robinson:

> *Within a week the classroom enrollment had dropped seventy-five percent. Protest that such would happen was fruitless: the directive was almost law. The persons who compiled it were the narrowest and most short sighted of the department, classic examples of bureaucratic stupidity, men who had never been out in the 'field,' who knew nothing of the actual operation of the program.*[74]

Thompson went on to argue that many of the classes already offered before the cut were the best suited to expose the prisoners to democratic principles, rather than the ones they were now being forced to offer. Many of the technical courses were "the best bait" the intelligence officers felt they had to draw prisoners to the program, an example being an engineering course into which "was injected the finest type of instruction in democracy."[75]

Because the mentality of those shaping the program came from a group of intellectuals, the program failed to utilize methods that might have better reached the ordinary soldier. This does not mean the program was incapable of communicating its ideas to the prisoners, but the fact that the intellectuals were over-enthusiastic at the prospect of feeding the prisoners a steady diet of academic thought crippled their judgment. Their methods were by no means a failure, but careful consideration of the suggestions from officers in the field would have led to a better understanding of how to best reach the average prisoner. As Ron Robin states, "It was, perhaps, quite unrealistic to assume than an introvert literary movement, however well-organized, could galvanize popular opposition to a totalitarian regime. Nevertheless, American authorities had great expectations from this select group of exiles."[76] Even if the program was the result of an "introvert literary movement," it still provided an enormous opportunity for German prisoners to be exposed to democracy.

How successful was the Intellectual Diversion Program? Did it succeed at changing the average German prisoner of war's view of America and democracy? Before we answer that question, it's imperative to see how the program actually worked in the camps, specifically the Nebraska POW camps.

PART II

THE NEBRASKA CAMPS

O ut of all the U.S. states, only five—Nevada, North Dakota, Rhode Island, Montana and Vermont—did not have POW camps. In Nebraska, there were three POW base camps—Camp Atlanta, located in Phelps County in south central Nebraska; Fort Robinson, located in northwest Nebraska in Dawes County; and Camp Scottsbluff, located in Scotts Bluff County in the Panhandle of Nebraska. Camp Indianola originally began in the summer of 1943 as a base camp, then was converted to a branch camp of Camp Atlanta in May 1944 and then once more became a base camp in September 1944. It ended the war as a branch camp of Camp Atlanta.

Camp Atlanta had approximately sixteen satellite or branch camps in the southern half of the state as well as two in Kansas. Between 1944 and 1945, they included Grand Island, Hastings, Kearney, Franklin, Hebron, Weeping Water, Elwood, Bertrand, Alma, Lexington, Palisade, Ogallala, Benkelman, Hayes Center and Indianola. The two in Kansas were at Hays and Cawker City.[77] Camp Scottsbluff, the oldest of the three base camps, had prisoners arrive in June 1943 and had branch camps at Bridgeport, Bayard, Lyman, Mitchell and Sidney, as well as two in Wyoming, Veteran and Torrington.[78] Italian prisoners were briefly interned at Fort Crook in Sarpy County near Omaha. With the exception of Fort Robinson, these camps were almost entirely used for agriculture and contract labor purposes.[79] In the fall of 1944, Fort Robinson had three side camps in South Dakota.[80]

CHAPTER 3

CAMP SCOTTSBLUFF

The Panhandle of western Nebraska is much different from the eastern portion of the state. Not only was it settled later than the east, but the climate is also much drier, humidity is rare and rainfall isn't as bountiful, making irrigation a necessity to farming. As part of the Great Plains, the landscape tends to run to long stretches of tree-less prairie, but there are beautiful rock formations that nature has carved out of clay and sandstone. Agriculture forms the bedrock of the economy, and main crops include sugar beets, dry edible beans, corn and wheat. Sugar beets were introduced into this region by the Germans from Russia and remain today one of the area's most profitable crops.

This region is also less populated than the eastern half of Nebraska. Scottsbluff, located in Scotts Bluff County, is still the largest community in the Platte Valley region, with a population of approximately fifteen thousand people. During the 1940s, the population was relatively the same. Because of the agriculture-based economy and the overall low population of the Panhandle region, Scottsbluff was also a natural choice for a POW camp.

Work began on January 26, 1943, at the former municipal airport located about five miles east of Scottsbluff off U.S. Highway 26. The prime contractors were Olson-Assemmacher-Rokahr and C.C. Larsen & Sons.[81] It followed the same construction plans as the other POW camps and was ready by June 1943 for its first prisoners. It had been activated in May 1943.

Right: A view of the Scotts Bluff National Monument in Scottsbluff, Nebraska. *Wikimedia Commons.*

Below: A view of Camp Scottsbluff from the camp's water tower. This is a typical layout of all POW camps that had to be built. *Legacy of the Plains Museum.*

THE AMERICAN PERSONNEL

American personnel changed frequently during the war. As of July 1944, Lieutenant Colonel Clyde B. Dempster was in charge of the Scottsbluff camp. Other key personnel included Adjutant Captain Clarence J. Powell, executive officer Major Richard Parnell and chaplain and representative for assistance to school Lieutenant Joseph Deleiden. Later personnel included Lieutenant L. Dude as assistant executive officer, Captain Fordyce as stockade officer and First Lieutenant Harold L. Brown as special services officer.[82]

The guard personnel at the camp had their own facilities. This included a game room with pool and Ping-Pong tables, furniture and a Coke machine; a reading room and study with what one report called "the best, in fact almost luxurious, furniture," as well as a radio phonograph with records; and a library that had around two thousand books and forty-six types of popular magazines

The U.S. officers' dining hall decorated for Thanksgiving at Camp Scottsbluff. *Legacy of the Plains Museum.*

and newspapers. The noncommissioned officers' club served 3.2 percent beer, and the jukebox furnished dance music.

H.J. Knoll noted in his 1945 report, "In leaving on furloughs American enlisted personnel may avail themselves of any government transportation going their way. In short, the Commanding Officer bestows on his men all possible benefits within his power." Knoll even said that Dempster's behavior toward the men should serve as a model to other camps suffering from low morale.[83]

Officers at Camp Scottsbluff during a Thanksgiving banquet. *Far left, across from table:* Lieutenant Pickerel and wife; *center table across:* Lieutenant Jim Green; *front left:* station surgeon (name unknown); *far right, this side of table:* Colonel Clyde B. Dempster and wife. *Legacy of the Plains Museum.*

THE ITALIANS

Scottsbluff's first prisoners weren't Germans but Italians captured from North Africa and Italy. Several hundred of them came to Scottsbluff in June 1943. According to a story that appeared in the local newspaper, the *Star-Herald*, most of the men were from the elite Italian rifle and sharpshooter units known as the *Bersaglieri*. These were not average soldiers but members of an exclusive corps of riflemen with a long, storied history stretching back to their creation by Captain Alessandro Ferrero De La Marmora in 1836 in the Kingdom of Piedmont-Sardinia. They wore distinctive black plumes on their helmets and earned an impressive reputation. Even German commander Erwin Rommel remarked, "The German soldier has impressed the world; however, the Italian *Bersagliere* soldier has impressed the German soldier."[84]

They were young, between twenty and twenty-five, and cut a fine figure to the reporters who wrote of their arrival. "And they are powerful men—broad shouldered, trim waisted and with smooth, strong muscles rippling beneath well bronzed skins. They are hard and fit—that's why they have been able to throw off the fatigue which they might well be expected to feel after long months of desert fighting."[85] Though they were no longer wearing their famous black plumes but torn and tattered clothing, they were a proud bunch all the same.

Herb Hinman, whose family lived across the road from the POW camp, remembers sitting with his family on their front porch and watching the Italians march into camp. "They seemed to be happy, some whistling or singing as they walked along like they were going for a stroll," he remembered. "They would even wave and speak out as they went by until the guards spoke to them."[86]

Records of when only the Italians were housed at Camp Scottsbluff are few and far between. Official inspection reports from the YMCA and Red Cross are hard to come by, thus leaving a gaping hole in what we can learn about this brief period.

Newspaper stories and personal recollections can give us a glimpse into the Italians' lives during their stay in the camp. Joe Fairfield, a boy at the time, thought the Italians were better suited to arts and crafts compared to the Germans. One prisoner, Rometi Pola, painted a mural on the inside of the camp administrator building that featured noted landmarks of the area, including Scotts Bluff National Monument, Court House and Jail Rock near Bridgeport and Chimney Rock by Bayard.[87]

Italian POWs at Camp Scottsbluff pose in front of their volleyball net with their mascot. *Legacy of the Plains Museum.*

The Italians were fairly content, though they did wish they could make spaghetti more often. The prisoners supplied their own cooks and did all of the work themselves around the compound. They had plenty of free time, and a favorite game to play was *bocce* ball, an ancient game similar to bowling.[88]

But on July 25, 1943, the labor shortage in rural Scottsbluff was about to get some relief. The War Department set up regulations for making prisoners of war available for farm labor, a welcome development considering harvest was just around the corner. Farmers who wanted laborers had to put in a request with their local county extension agent. The minimum amount of prisoners for each group was ten. Once the request was approved, the farmers were instructed to pick up the prisoners at the camp, as well as the guard. Farmers had to pay the cost of guarding the prisoners and provide the tools necessary to get the job done. They were not required to provide lunch to the prisoners, who would have sandwiches, but they did need to provide drinking water. The farmer paid whatever the prevailing local wage for similar work was at the time, which would be given to the POWs in the form of canteen coupons to use at the POW camp. In addition, the farmer could not live more than an hour away from the camp.[89] Later, side camps, or branch camps, were set up in smaller towns around Scottsbluff to reduce travel time.

For A.J. Williams, who was eight years old in 1943, the Italian POWs were a welcome diversion. His family needed help harvesting the potato crop. "The Italians didn't work all that fast," he remembered. "But we were grateful for whatever help we could get." One of the Italians turned out to have been a cab driver in the Bronx before the war. He went back to Rome to take care of some family business and ended up drafted into the Italian army. One day, this same POW asked the farmer if they could take a different route to the farm, one that would go past anywhere there might be girls. "So after work that day," Williams recalled, "the truck left a little early and went past the college, the hospital, and the high school. There were plenty of girls, and plenty of whistles, waves and shouts from the POWs. Dad was happy, too. He'd found the secret of getting the men to work."[90]

Of course, it wasn't all work and no play. Joe Fairfield remembered an amusing, if slightly alarming, incident that happened on their farm, located within a half mile of the North Platte River west of Minatare. A prisoner thought the river might be an excellent hunting ground. "One of the prisoners asked to use the guard's gun, to go down on the river for awhile. Evidently he must have been well trusted, as the guard let him use his gun," Fairfield recalled.

"Shortly afterward the P.O.W. came back with pheasant feathers sticking in his cap, and turned the gun back over to the guard."[91]

Williams also recalled an incident in which the Italian POWs were using a guard's rifle. He came home from school and heard shots being fired. He thought perhaps an escape was in progress, but the truth wasn't nearly as exciting. "The guard, Dad and the POWs were celebrating the end of the potato harvest by using the guard's rifle to determine who was the best marksman," Williams said. "The targets— extra sunburned potatoes— exploded as they were hit."[92]

To read such amusing anecdotes might give the impression that the Italian

Two U.S. servicemen stand in front of Camp Scottsbluff's post office. *Legacy of the Plains Museum.*

POWs' life in America was idyllic, and to some extent, it was. It was certainly much better than being on the battlefield.

On September 8, 1943, Italy surrendered and soon declared war on Germany. Suddenly, the War Department had to determine what to do with all of the Italian POWs being kept in America. Italy had a new status, that of a cobelligerent. But this didn't mean the Italian POWs were free to go. Instead, the government continued to take care of the prisoners according to the Geneva Convention and allowed them to be employed on projects directly related to military operations via a parole system. Just because the Italians were now on the Allied side didn't mean all of the Italian POWs expressed anti-fascist tendencies. Those who qualified for the parole program had been certified as trustworthy after a lengthy time of observation by the Americans.[93]

Farmers were worried that their source of labor might dry up. Documents show just how much the farmers had come to rely on the POWs for agricultural purposes. The Scotts Bluff County Labor Board president, Fred M. Atteberry, sent an urgent telegram to U.S. congressman A.L. Miller of Nebraska's Fourth Legislative District in February 1944. Rumors had reached the county labor board that the War Department intended to remove the Italian prisoners of war from the Scottsbluff camp. This would wreak havoc, Atteberry said. "Our whole crop production program depends upon an adequate supply of farm labor being available and the prisoners of war have been counted upon to supply a portion of this labor," he wrote. Miller received a reply from Lieutenant Colonel Horatio R. Rogers, the executive to the assistant to the provost marshal general, stating, "At the present time, there are no plans to move the Italian prisoners of war now interned at that installation." Furthermore, if the War Department did plan to transfer the Italian PWs, arrangements would be made to make sure German POWs filled the labor gap.[94]

The Italians had another option besides staying in the camp or working at a factory. They could join the Italian Service Units (ISUs). In October 1943, the OPMG suggested creating a labor division made up of volunteer Italian PWs who were not fascists, had passed a screening test and were in full cooperation with the program. The men received either training at a specialized camp or had on-the-job training. These labor units would work on anything that would further the war effort. But complications arose, including the language barrier and the need to translate technical manuals. The program didn't go into effect until the spring of 1944. However, at the end of the war, the program was deemed a success, "releasing U.S. service personnel for overseas duties."[95]

But some Italian POWs who wanted to volunteer for ISUs faced trouble inside the POW camps. At Camp Scottsbluff, Ferruccio Piccolo circulated a letter to his fellow Italian soldiers in March 1944 that urged them to stay true to Italy, despite its surrender in September 1943 and despite the collapse of its fascist government.[96]

Piccolo, who signed the letter as the "Chief of Company," wrote:

A measure of calm has followed the tormented days of this past week. A certain unity of intentions has been reached because now we can look each other in the eye and freely expound our sentiments of love of country without touching the susceptibilities of the unfortunes [sic] past companions of ours who have not hesitated to choose the path which is not that of honor...Perhaps the attempts to bend us have not yet been ended. We must remain intractable. Even should we be detached and separated we promise ourselves, and to our friends and to our companions that we shall not yield…Courage and decision, dear Comrades. LONG LIVE ITALY.[97]

But the letter wasn't the only thing that pointed the authorities at Camp Scottsbluff to these men's political persuasions. The army had compiled a list of men who'd committed grievances against other Italian POWS. Most complaints consisted of pro-fascist Italian POWs threatening anti-fascist Italian POWs with harm to them or their families if they signed up for ISUs. According to the document, they also "intimidated said prisoners by telling them that their families will also be punished in Italy." This same group of approximately thirty-eight men was "considered to represent more than mere organized resistance against the formation of Italian Service Units, and many apparently should have been earmarked in the initial screening."[98]

Unfortunately, there were those who slipped through the cracks. During the screening process, it was simply impossible to accurately judge a man's political motivations unless he was vocal and outspoken about it. However, fascism in the camps wasn't nearly as big of a problem as Nazism.

Regardless of whether or not these thirty-eight particular Italian POWs at Scottsbluff were truly dangerous and intended to do harm to others, they were summarily transferred to the prisoner of war camp in Hereford, Texas, where nearly all Italian fascists were housed during the war.[99]

However, it is unclear as to when the Italian POWs in Scottsbluff were repatriated back to Italy. Though there were still Italian POWs in the camp as late as the spring of 1944, the rest of the records are strangely silent on their presence. Perhaps the arrival of the Germans eclipsed all else.

THE GERMANS

Many of the German POWS who first came to Scottsbluff and filled two compounds were members of General Erwin Rommel's elite *Afrika Korps* who had served in Tunisia, Algeria and Libya. Others had served in Italy. Some had previously been interred at Camp Trinidad in Colorado. And they weren't all of German ethnicity, either. Because of Hitler's wide swathe of conquered countries, men from Poland, Czechoslovakia, Austria, Yugoslavia and even Switzerland were interned at Scottsbluff. The archives are full of letters from these men asking to be transferred to camps where the Nazi presence wasn't prevalent since they were very particular targets.

Thus, with this conglomeration of ethnicities and differing political beliefs, the German soldiers who showed up in Scottsbluff, Nebraska, in May 1944 gave a far different impression than had the Italians. Douglas Stanton, who wrote the story for the *Star-Herald* newspaper about the Italian POWs when they first arrived, couldn't fail to notice the difference between the two armies when he wrote about the camp in June 1944. "The Nazis at the Scottsbluff Prisoner of War Camp are a breed of men showing little in common with the Italians who preceded them," Stanton wrote. "In fact, the vivacious, buoyant and voluble southern Europeans who recently moved out, form a perfect contrast to the reserved, taciturn Teutons who have moved in."[100]

Rudolf Ritschel, a German soldier who was taken prisoner in Cassino, Italy, recalled his experience arriving at the Scottsbluff POW camp.

> *After the arrival at PW-Camp Scottsbluff, each of us felt the greatest amazement concerning the reception at that midnight hour. In the mess hall the tables were set and a meal was brought out, such as we had not seen for a long time. Every man received a duffle bag with clothing and underwear. What probably nobody had dared believe before was reality. We slept as prisoners of war in beds with white sheets. After a thorough medical examination, a four-week period of rest was prescribed.*[101]

There is some dispute over the period of rest, which was more akin to being quarantined. One former German POW later remembered, "The hardest part was the first six weeks. They quarantined us. We couldn't get out and work like the others," he said. "I remember that young girls would come by from the city and bring us cookies and apples. We asked why they were bringing us these things. They said that they wanted to see the 'Nazis.'"[102]

Stanton's article is the best source on life for the Germans in that first month or so in the camp. He reported that many could speak or understand some English, and one of the first things they noted upon arrival was the lack of trees and flowerbeds around the camp. They promptly remedied this by planting a flower and vegetable garden. The POWs also organized themselves well into kitchen, hospital and police details. They furnished their own cooks, who baked "fine soft bread" at the rate of a ton of bread a day under the supervision of an American mess sergeant. They also made sure each prisoner had his own birthday cake on his birthday. Like most servicemen, the Germans decorated their barracks with pinup girls and family photographs.

But perhaps the most striking difference between the Italian POWs and the German POWs was the professional distance the Germans showed toward their captors. "Their every action shows they are proud men, strong soldiers who have been captured but have lost not one iota of their self respect," Stanton wrote. "They don't smile, and they look grim. Yet these Nazis don't give the impression of being sullen or vindictive. They are formally polite. Most of all they are aloof."[103]

By late July, men from Normandy arrived and composed the third compound. These men showed a marked difference to Rommel's proud *Afrika Corps*. Not only were they much older than their comrades, but they also "were not so 'cocky' as the Afrika Korspmen," M.W. Downle, a reporter for the *Star-Herald*, wrote. "Those from Normandy were dead tired, war weary and poorly clothed."[104] Upon an inspection tour of the camp July 29–30, 1944, a representative of the YMCA also observed the difference in these new prisoners from Normandy:

> *The sudden pall of prison camp also is evident. As I took pictures one late afternoon following supper, I was struck by something the camera could not catch except in closeups, which I did not wish to take. All along the inner compound fence were the new men, some talking with older prisoners, others aimlessly walking to and fro. All the new men were still dressed in their soiled, wrinkled uniforms, looking somewhat like Emperor Jones in his second-hand lodge pageantry, somewhat pathetic in their tarnished military finery.*[105]

Herb Hinman also recalled the difference between the first Germans who arrived at Scottsbluff with those from Normandy. "The first few loads [of German prisoners] were very brisk, marching like on parade and very arrogant acting," he said. "I remember that at least once or twice they were singing some kind of marching song…Later, the German prisoners became much more bedraggled looking and not disciplined like the first and it seemed to me they were much younger, too."[106]

Regardless of age, POWs were needed for work, and due to the severe labor shortage in the summer of 1944, these Germans were about to be put to the test.

LABOR

The Scottsbluff POW camp was like a miniature community and operated much the same way. There were tailors and shoe repairmen, bakers, engineer

German POW bakers and American servicemen pose with pies for the Thanksgiving banquet. Servicemen, *from left to right:* James Loy, Captain Smith and Nickolette Olie. *Legacy of the Plains Museum.*

details, hospital workers and kitchen police, just to name a few. There was never a shortage of work to do inside the camp. But the majority of POWs were needed outside the barbed-wire fence.

In 1944, according to Brigadier General Paul B. Clemens, director of the Seventh Service Command security and intelligence division, "requests for P.O.W. labor are running between six and seven times the number available." Those who wanted to use POW labor had to go to his or her state extension director and see what the current wages were in the area, get a certificate of need and then give the application to the state or regional War Manpower Commission director. The service command would then "determine the requirements for suitable housing, transportation, sanitation, security, etc. at the site of the project, and whether POW labor may be properly employed." If the petitioner survived this somewhat lengthy process and his application was approved, he would then be given the use of the POWs—if there were any available.[107]

Lois Neeley's father went through this process to build a large equipment shed. Though he only needed one or two extra men, the minimum he could take was six. So, while a few POWs helped him pour and level the concrete floor and build and erect the frames for the walls, the others spent their time in quite a different way. "The ones not working on the shed entertained my little sister and I by clowning around and by goose stepping around the yard, doing the Heil Hitler salute, mocking the German army," Lois recalls.[108]

Soon, German POWs could be found working in the fields around Scottsbluff and neighboring towns. Branch camps were eventually set up in these towns to ease transportation and housing issues. However, that didn't mean everyone was happy about the enemy working nearby. "Gen. Clemens said that while there is still resentment against POW labor in a few localities, the demand for it at this time is traceable to past success," the *Star-Herald* reported. In addition, there was nothing on record for attempted sabotage or violence at any of the labor camps.

In fact, most firsthand accounts say nothing about problems between the farmers and the POWs and more often than not speak to the good relations between the two. One German POW recalled, "The farmers said that we worked hard. They were especially nice to us but they weren't allowed to feed us. One farmer didn't think we were being fed enough to work all day the way we did so he brought us a big lunch every day. We told him that this wasn't allowed but he said, 'Let them bring a hundred officers. I only fear God.'" This same farmer also arranged with the guards at the Scottsbluff camp to let the POWs spend the entire day at his house. "We were there between 8 in the morning and 4 in the afternoon," the former POW remembered. "It was not a holiday, but it was a day of celebration for us. For eight hours we weren't prisoners, we were just people visiting the house of a farmer."[109]

Rudolf Ritschel also had good things to say about those farmers who employed him and his fellow prisoners. "I was often a guest for dinner in the homes of farmers of German origin," he recalled. "Each of them was interested in talking with the German boys some time."[110]

As a boy, Wilbert Ruppel lived with his family on a farm about one mile north of the POW camp. He and his father would drive their 1938 Ford truck down to the camp to pick up prisoners to thin beets, weed crops and, in the fall, pick potatoes. They would have as many as twenty to twenty-five prisoners working for them, along with two guards. "We never, ever had any problem with those prisoners," he recalls. "They were all real nice guys. My folks were German and they could communicate with them. They all enjoyed talking with each other even though they were enemies." Ruppel remembered one instance in particular when a prisoner put two hands under his arms and lifted him into the air. "He had tears running down his cheeks," Ruppel recalls. "I didn't understand it then, but I do now. Maybe he had a son at home."

Like other farm families, the Ruppels fed home-cooked meals to the prisoners. "My parents always cooked them a noon meal, mashed potatoes and gravy and roast beef or pork chops. They fed the guards also. They really appreciated that. They all ate under the trees."[111] It also appeared that just about everyone didn't mind the rules being bent, especially when considering that an article appeared in the *Star-Herald* with the headline, "Nazi Prisoner Sheds Tears as Gets Fine Food in Farm Home." A German POW from Scottsbluff was working in Worland, Wyoming, as part of a group of POWs working in the beet fields. He was weeding a vegetable garden, and for lunch on their last day, the farm wife served fried chicken, fresh vegetables, ice cream and cake. The story stated, "A blond, chisel-featured Nazi, once a non-commissioned officer, was visibly affected. Near the end of the meal he lowered his head and cried. When he left he kissed the farmer's small son, said someday he would bring his young daughter to America to visit—or live if he were permitted. A Nazi lieutenant said it was the first time in five years the man had shown any emotion."[112]

It wasn't unheard of for the POWs and the farmers to join in conversation with each other, either. Herb Hinman recalled one conversation he had about the quality of the soil in America compared to Germany. "One of them told me quite arrogantly that the farm land in Germany was much better than ours because they didn't have to irrigate it and it was better soil anyway," Hinman remembers. "As a kid [eighteen at the time] I kind of resented his attitude, not understanding how he must have felt being a prisoner and having to do work that maybe he didn't have to do at home."[113]

One farmer trusted the POWs enough to leave his wife at home alone with them while he took his tractor over to help a neighbor. "Their speech was low and guttural which made them sound more harsh and frightening," Mrs. E.B. Fairfield recalled in 1978, "but all went well even when I had to let two or three come into the kitchen to get drinking water." Not only did Mrs. Fairfield supply the men with a cold drink on a hot summer day, but she was also able to get rid of some jelly that she'd planned to toss.

I enjoyed making jelly and jam, yet had learned that others than me in the family didn't care for it as I did, and [I] had lots of the jars on the table, thinking to throw it out. Some were several years old and rather sugary. One POW noticed them, called it marmalade, made motions in asking for it. I was glad to get rid of it, and every jar was returned, completely cleaned out even if I hadn't spoons enough. Then they gathered in formation with one acting as leader and marched back to work as they had come.[114]

Mrs. Fairfield also helped one of the POWs smuggle a kitten into the camp. Since the prisoners were punished if they were thought to have stolen anything while out on work detail, Mrs. Fairfield asked one of the guards for help. Yes, pets were allowed inside the camp, the guard said, but food for the pets had to come from the POWs own rations. So Mrs. Fairfield did the only thing she could: "I gave them a kitten, of course, as we always had more than we wanted."[115]

After their initial reluctance at hiring enemy soldiers, the local farmers now depended on the German POWs to help with harvest. Without them, crops would rot in the fields. Even after Germany surrendered in May 1945, farmers wanted the POWs to stay as long as possible to help with the harvest. Their labor efforts had not gone unnoticed. Figures compiled showed that they had harvested about "2,201,243 bushels of potato crop—estimated at 5,250,000 bushels, and topped approximately 12,758 acres of beets in Scotts Bluff and the southern part of Sioux County."

Of course, the POWs didn't just work. During their off-hours, the POW camp had plenty of recreational opportunities to keep them occupied.

DAILY LIFE AT THE CAMP

When the prisoners arrived at the camp, they wasted no time settling in. They built shelves over their bunks and hung pinups (apparently popular with men the world over, as both the Germans and the Italians had them). Photos of loved ones and pictures of home also surrounded the men as they tried to make their new quarters as much of a home as possible.

A "Safety Pays" sign at Camp Scottsbluff reminds everyone how accidents can hinder work productivity. *Legacy of the Plains Museum.*

They also ate well. Doris Steele worked in the food distribution department of the camp. "There were times we would switch the menu because the menu for the POWs was better than what the soldiers were getting," she remembered.[116]

The prisoners were free to read books, watch films, participate in sporting events, worship and even produce and act in plays and skits. All in all, it was a comfortable way to spend the remainder of the war.

Religion

Despite their fascist governments, many German and Italian POWs were religious. There was plenty of evidence to show that most of the Italian POWs were staunch Roman Catholics. One of the Italians' first projects was building an altar in the camp chapel. Religious pictures of the Blessed Virgin and other Catholic symbols also dotted their bunks, having survived the Africa campaign.[117]

When the Germans arrived, they had their own pinup gals, of course, along with other pictures "apparently clipped from German magazines," but they did not put their religion on display as did the Italians.[118]

The camp itself had a chapel within a barracks-type building. According to an inspection report, "The Italian legacy is the altar and the work of the Germans has been to make good benches out of scrap lumber. The P.W. pastor has a study at one end." To accommodate all the men in the camp, four services were held, two Catholic and two Lutheran. Attendance was usually good. One Lutheran service struck a chord with the visiting inspector as he related how the prisoners sang the hymn "A Mighty Fortress Is Our God" at the end. "I wondered what they were thinking, of what any prisoner of war would think of, as they sang the final stanza," he wrote.[119] In addition to the Sunday services, there was a midweek Bible study as well as a prayer hour.

In February 1945, however, a visiting reporter noted that more of the POWs had turned to religion to deal with the all-too-plausible idea that the Reich would soon be defeated. Church attendance rose. "Once many of them spurned the philosophy and comforts of the church as a sign of weakness," M.W. Downle wrote, "but it is different now. There are some holdouts, but the chapel is full for services."[120] Official government documents broke down the religious affiliations of the German POWs at

Scottsbluff thusly: 42 percent Catholic, 53 percent Protestant (Lutheran) and 3 percent called themselves "Believers-in-God," while 2 percent had no religious preference.[121]

Pastor Carl Gustaf Almquist from the World Council of Churches visited the camp along with YMCA inspector Howard Hong in early July 1945. He left a detailed report of his impressions of the camp that corroborates the increased religious mood. He wrote:

> *It was impossible to be mistaken that I met among these four* [POW] *pastors a seriousness and enthusiasm for their work to the benefit of their comrades…every morning, praying to God and reading the Scriptures, they tried to find out God's will for them for that very day, and what they could do for their comrades who had not yet become Christians. The pastors were really and deeply convinced men, who wanted to be ambassadors of God in the camp and some day at home, if God so wished.*

Almquist also reported that these pastors believed the German Church could help bring about a "Christian revival among the German people."[122]

After the relentless onslaught of Nazi propaganda that sought to eliminate Christianity from the nation, this was a tall order but not an impossible one.

MUSIC AND THEATER

Music and theater became a way for many men to bring a sense of normalcy to their lives, as well as find enrichment and entertainment. Prisoners were allowed to have radios (long-wave only) and often listened to music programs. The Germans formed a brass band shortly after their arrival. Some prisoners had managed to bring their instruments with them, having carried them during the war. In later months, there emerged a camp orchestra to entertain the men. Incredibly, a former first violinist of the Vienna Philharmonic orchestra was one of the POWs, and he led the camp's string quintet in July 1944.[123] The orchestra played concerts in the theater during the winter and performed outdoors in the summer.

Using funds from the YMCA, prisoners purchased orchestral instruments from local merchants. The thirty-four-piece orchestra performed "light opera and light concert music" and was quite eager to learn American music, as well.[124] During his visit to the camp in July 1945,

d the POW orchestra playing a concert at the camp
mrades.[125]
Italians lost no time in establishing a theater in what the
r termed "the opera house," but the Germans were not
impressed with their decorating and tore down their "ornate trappings."[126]
Howard Hong reported in December 1944 that the lack of space made it
difficult to put on theatrical productions, but at least there was interest in the
endeavor. By late January 1945, however, the prisoners had yet to put on a
play.[127] Whether this changed is unknown.

RECREATION AND ARTS AND CRAFTS

Exercise of the body and the mind was also an important consideration in
the life of the POW. Accordingly, a variety of leisure activities was offered
for the prisoners, from handicrafts to sports. Painting, woodcarving and
other arts and crafts were more popular during the winter months when
farm labor was no longer available.

Steve Sorok, a former U.S. serviceman at the camp, remembered how the
Italians much preferred handcrafts to labor. "The Italians liked to work more or
less with their hands, and [were] musically inclined. The Germans were more
active physically."[128] The Germans, however, still did their share of handcrafts.
Painting, woodcarving and woodburning were popular activities, as was
clay modeling. To fuel the men's enthusiasm, a winter hobby exhibition and
competition with YMCA-provided prizes was proposed and eagerly embraced
by the commanding officer and camp leaders alike.[129] Some of the POWs' work
is on display at the Legacy of the Plains Museum in Gering, Nebraska.

Interestingly enough, in the spring of 1945, when Hitler's demise was
inevitable, the German prisoners began making suitcases. "Whether this is
a symptom of the annually recurrent wanderlust induced by spring fever,"
Major Neuland wrote in his inspection report, "or whether it is a reflection
of their belief in the imminence of V-E Day, is not quite clear."[130]

Other activities included chess tournaments, music lessons and gardening.
In fact, seven acres were set aside and broken into 1,800 garden plots.[131]

One activity both the Germans and the Italians had a common passion
for was sports. The Italians enjoyed playing *bocci* or *bocce* ball, a bowling game
similar to one played by the ancient Romans. Both Italians and Germans
played soccer, volleyball and handball. As one reporter put it, "They like

Right: Italian POWs play *bocce* ball at Camp Scottsbluff. *Legacy of the Plains Museum.*

Below: Italian POWs play a rousing game of volleyball while one POW decides to pose for another photo with the camp mascot. *Legacy of the Plains Museum.*

to stay outdoors and soak up the sunshine." Outdoor games were played on two nearby fields, and for indoor games, five rooms were used in the recreation hall. Ping-Pong was also a favorite game for the Germans. One report noted that the German POWs also had boxing equipment and a ring, but it was rarely used since "the sportsleader is a soccer enthusiast with little interest in diversified activities."[132]

Intellectual diversions, however, were just as eagerly embraced as the recreational ones.

Education

During a time of war, when one thinks of being held prisoner in a foreign country by one's enemy, one doesn't usually think that it would include educational classes. Recreation, hobbies and labor are understandable. But classes on biology, geography or mathematics? Yet these classes—and more—were offered to the POWs. Whether the POWs elected to attend classes or not was entirely up to them, but many took advantage of the chance to educate themselves.

In July 1944, the Scottsbluff camp already had a good educational program with the help of a POW who'd been a high school teacher. Classes were offered in biology, geography, mathematics, French, English, German, stenography and history. There were approximately 950 men registered for these courses, a not insignificant amount. Camp authorities and the prisoners alike were interested in starting a correspondence courses program.[133]

Books were provided by the YMCA, the International Committee of the Red Cross and even the German Red Cross. By the time the Intellectual Diversion Program was put into place, there were 2,418 books in the POW library with a staggering 70 percent "in constant circulation."[134]

The Intellectual Diversion Program at Scottsbluff

Camp Scottsbluff commander Colonel Dempster was "squarely behind the reorientation program in all of its phases." He worked closely with Lieutenant Browne, the assistant executive officer in charge of the program. According to official reports, Lieutenant Brown had done a remarkable job easing his way into the position. Since the reeducation program was top secret, it remained imperative that the German POWs were unaware of the fact that they were, essentially, being taught the benefits of democracy in order to "de-Nazify" them.[135]

Lieutenant Browne made significant changes to the education and leisure programs already in place. He increased the orchestra's presence, started a theater group, improved the selection of magazines and newspapers and even organized a hobby competition and athletic carnival with prizes.

More notably, however, Lieutenant Browne had identified those "subversive leaders" within the ranks of the German POWs who had every intention of sabotaging the program. These individuals were well known to the German

POW informers, men who gladly passed on intelligence information to the Americans. However, giving the Americans the names of these potential subversives was different. They feared retribution and rightly so. As pointed out earlier, there were numerous incidents of Nazi persecution among the POW camps.[136]

The course offerings the men had been taking changed when the Intellectual Diversion Program was implemented at Scottsbluff. In fact, many parts of the men's lives were affected as the War Department sought to show the prisoners how democracy was far superior to Nazism.

In March 1945, twelve prisoners became instructors, headed by the director of studies, thirty-eight-year-old POW Obergefreiter Horst Weinhold of Saxony, Germany. Though these men did not know about the reeducation program, all of them were carefully scrutinized to make sure they would not be detrimental to the program's success. This included sitting in on classroom discussions, interviewing them and even using informers. By utilizing these tools and staying diligent, the higher-ups were convinced that the camp didn't need any further "resources" to weed out subversives.[137]

Most of the men were interested in technical and scientific courses. A sample of some of the books the camp ordered from Barnes & Noble in New York bears this out. Books included *Logarithmic and Trigonometry Tables*, *Chemical Calculations*, *Organic Chemistry* and *Industrial Fabrics*. Other books were geared toward language and the fine arts. The *English-German Dictionary*, *It's Fun to Draw* and *Modern American Painting* were also on the list.[138]

The reeducation program used the classroom to subtly (and sometimes not so subtly) educate the Germans on the superiority of democracy compared to Nazism. Surprisingly, they also used motion pictures.

MOTION PICTURES

Nothing captured the POWs' imaginations quite like American films. At Camp Scottsbluff, films were available in sixteen millimeter and thirty-five millimeter and were shown on Sunday and Monday afternoons. There were no subtitles, of course, and the POWs had to rely on a short synopsis written by their camp spokesman to understand the films' plots. They apparently enjoyed musicals, especially those in color, as well as westerns. Most films were given a cursory look to see if they contained anything controversial or dealt with Nazism. But this process changed when the Intellectual Diversion Program began.[139]

Some German-language films were selected to show the prisoners, but they were carefully screened to make sure they contained no Nazi propaganda. Lieutenant Browne also screened every picture before it was shown, as did the camp spokesman and the director of the educational studies program.[140]

By February 1945, the camp had three sixteen-millimeter projectors. This made it possible for the movie to run continuously through the day, allowing more POWs to attend. Lieutenant Browne made a significant change in the type of movies shown to the POWs. In addition to more popular fare, he added educational films on the United States, including those on "various phases of American industry."[141]

Browne wrote to several companies, including General Electric in New York, asking if they had any educational films on their industries. However, none of the film footage could be "derogatory to the war effort."[142] Lieutenant Browne was also encouraged to contact someone within the sugar beet industry to see if he could obtain a film about this staple of the Panhandle's farming economy. Such a film would help orient POWs who would be laboring in the fields in the spring of 1945.[143]

Unfortunately, we do not have records to tell us just how successful the Intellectual Diversion Program was at Scottsbluff. Indeed, the question of the reeducation program's success overall throughout the United States is difficult to measure.

CAMP SCOTTSBLUFF AFTER THE WAR

Even though the war in Europe ended on May 8, 1945, the German POWs were not immediately returned home. The process of repatriating them to their country would take months, and prisoners wouldn't go home until mid-1946 or later. Most certainly, some did not *want* to go home, especially those who would be returning to what was now known as East Germany and a Communist government under the Soviet Union.

Local farmers weren't eager to see their cheap labor force leave, either. The war with Japan was still raging, and who knew when the American boys would come home? Even after Japan was defeated and 1945 stretched into 1946, farmers still needed the labor. The Scotts Bluff County Farm Labor Board estimated it would need around 3,400 POWs and around 1,000

Another view of Camp Scottsbluff from the water tower. Notice how close local farms were to the camp. *Legacy of the Plains Museum.*

"Mexican nationals" for the sugar beet harvest.[144] But many of the POWs were transferred to camps in Colorado or to the West Coast "for shipment to Europe by way of the Panama canal."[145]

After the last man left in the spring of 1946, Camp Scottsbluff was dismantled. Some buildings were bought by local businesses or farmers and hauled away. The administrative building, with colorful murals on the walls painted by the Italians, became the American Legion Hall in the nearby town of Minatare. After the camp had been dismantled, all that remained was the cement foundations. The City of Scottsbluff began using the area as a city dump.[146]

But there were many POWs who wanted to make their home in Scottsbluff. After going home to Germany, they put the wheels in motion for their eventual returns to America. For some, it took years. Werner Prautzsch applied for immigration in 1947, and four years later, he and his wife, Erika, came to America in 1950 and 1951, respectively, under the sponsorship of Herman Gompert, a local farmer Werner had worked for while a prisoner. Prautzsch settled in the Mitchell area and retired in 2001 from the DeKalb Seed Corn business.[147]

Others returned to visit. Sergio Bologna was an Italian POW at Scottsbluff and came to visit in April 1999. His wife accompanied him, and in a story for the *Star-Herald*, she was quoted as saying, "He has no hate or resentment. He says the experience [of being a prisoner] was part of his growth. And he says the past has to help create the future."[148]

CHAPTER 4

CAMP ATLANTA

About thirty-eight miles south of Kearney on Highway 183 sits the small town of Holdrege. A few miles before the town appears, there is a museum with a guard tower reminiscent of those used at Camp Atlanta more than seventy years ago. This is the Nebraska Prairie Museum, and it is filled with historical goodness. Of particular interest is a fairly new section of the museum expressly dedicated to the POW camp. It includes camp relics; the Thomas F. Naegele Gallery, an art exhibit by noted artist, Thomas F. Naegele, who was stationed at Camp Indianola and later, Camp Atlanta; uniforms; and all manner of miscellaneous items. Local author Glenn Thompson wrote the definitive history of the camp in *Prisoners on the Plains*.

The tiny village of Atlanta, population of 173 according to the 1940 census,[149] is located approximately eight miles from Holdrege in Phelps County, Nebraska. A plot of three hundred acres of land a few miles from the village, between Holdrege and Atlanta, was picked to build the camp.

It is amusing to see how the different camp inspectors described this region. Paul Schnyer from the International Red Cross said, "The region is flat and monotonous. The only trees to be seen are those which were planted around the camp. The climate is warm with rather cool nights. The region is greatly exposed to wind."[150] But Swiss Legation representative Charles C. Eberhardt described it differently. "This camp is situated in the gently rolling and fertile uplands of south-central Nebraska, a prosperous agricultural community which even without irrigation usually produces bountiful crops of corn and wheat."[151]

The entrance to the Camp Atlanta POW Exhibit at Nebraska Prairie Museum in Holdrege, Nebraska. *Author photo.*

This mural, painted by Mark Marcuson of Lincoln, Nebraska, greets the visitor at the entrance to the Camp Atlanta POW Exhibit at Nebraska Prairie Museum in Holdrege, Nebraska. *Author photo.*

Those "bountiful crops" were one of the main reasons the government chose this area for the camp's location. Agriculture was (and still is) the area's main industry, with crops such as wheat, corn, potatoes and sugar beets (introduced in 1942 here), as well as a thriving livestock industry. But planting and harvesting crops to feed America and the boys overseas couldn't be done unless there were men to do it. The severe labor shortage threatened to leave many crops rotting in the field.

At first, the proposed camp was meant to be for conscientious objectors to help out with the labor shortage. But then came the deal with the British to take POWs, and suddenly, the camp became an ideal location for a POW camp. This announcement came in May 1942, shocking the residents of Holdrege and Atlanta. The general fears of mass escape, sabotage and the fact that the enemy would be right outside their front doors held little appeal for many. But the dire need for labor trumped all objections.[152]

The camp was built quickly, following the general blueprints drawn up by the War Department. By the time it was activated as part of the Seventh Service Command in October 1943, there were around two hundred buildings, including a huge water tower. It had three compounds, each with the capacity to hold one thousand prisoners.

Swiss representative Eberhardt gives perhaps one of the best descriptions of the camp:

> *Each compound is supplied with the usual barracks, messhalls, canteen, lavatories, and other buildings to accommodate one thousand men. The buildings are constructed of composition known as granule which is said to be more comfortable for inmates both in summer and in winter than any camp buildings formerly constructed. The floors are all made of cement and the ceilings are covered with water-proof roofing. The buildings are furnished with stoves in which coal is used for fuel. In the barracks double deck metal beds are used and all buildings appear to have plenty of light and air and are not at all overcrowded.[153]*

Eberhardt found the barracks so well arranged that he asked for a photograph. He considered them a "model for neatness and comfortable arrangement."[154]

The camp was put under the command of Lieutenant Colonel Leonard R. Smith and made ready for the influx of U.S. soldiers, civilian workers and, later, the German POWs. American soldiers started arriving along with civilian workers, and soon, the little town of Holdrege became a hive of activity.

In October 1943, the War Department released a statement to all area newspapers, and suddenly, the fact that Germans were to be interred on Nebraska soil became a stark reality. The statement gave instructions on "a need for constant vigilance." Firearms were to be locked up, and "cars with engines running should not be left unattended and ignition keys should be removed." Keeping men's clothing on clotheslines overnight or keeping them in an outbuilding was forbidden since escaped POWs would have the opportunity to steal them and thus blend in with the locals. To make the POWs easy to spot, their new clothing would have the letters "PW" on the sleeves of jackets and shirts and on the trousers above the knee.[155]

THE AMERICAN PERSONNEL

In May 1944, the American personnel listed on the Department of State and the Swiss Legation report included commander Lieutenant Colonel Leonard R. Smith, adjutant and executive officer Captain Loren E. Ellis, internal security officer Major Thomas R. McCarthy, stockade officer Captain Clifford G. Ashmore, medical officer Major Kenneth E. Lister and chaplain First Lieutenant Harry F. Shoaf.[156]

Most American military personnel lived in Holdrege, but there were some posted at the camp itself. The camp also employed a large contingent of civilian employees. With the influx of people, Holdrege officially became a military town, and a housing shortage soon appeared. A bus route, the Chet Conn Bus Line, was established between Holdrege and the camp so that soldiers and camp employees didn't have to walk the six miles to work or waste precious rationed gasoline.[157]

Unfortunately, as noted in a memorandum from Major Paul A. Neuland, the guards at Camp Atlanta suffered from the same problems as guards at other camps around the nation. In short, they were incompetent to a large degree, something that the camp commander noticed. "Lieutenant Colonel Smith considers the appearance, attitude, and the morale of his guard as unsatisfactory," Neuland reported. "The transfer of one-third overseas soldiers into his guard personnel has been detrimental. These men for the most part are mentally unstable and what he terms 'trigger happy.'" Neuland went on to say that most of these men had to be discharged and that the "sullen" guards were making a terrible impression upon the German POWs.[158]

THE PRISONERS ARRIVE

Despite the camp being ready in 1943, the first German prisoners didn't arrive at Atlanta until January 25, 1944, three months behind schedule. These prisoners had been in Camp Concordia, Kansas, and were being transferred to Atlanta to help work in the camp and relieve the American military from this duty. The second group of POWs arrived by train on January 27 and came straight from the front in North Africa. A third group arrived in March 1944.[159]

The detailed report from the Swiss Legation in May 1944 broke down the prisoners by country of origin: 1,223 Germans, 147 Austrians, 38 from the Sudentenland, 29 Polish, one Dutchman, one man from Switzerland and four Italians. The report also had glowing reviews for the camp personnel and how well the camp was run. "[Mr. Tobler] stated…that Camp Atlanta stands high in his estimation among our best administered prisoner of war camps. The writer concurs unreservedly in this sentiment."[160]

In 1945, the Camp Atlanta newspaper for the U.S. soldiers summed up what turned out to be a monumental task:

> Since January 1944 in mud and rain, over fifty groups of PWs have marched up "Nebraska Avenue" into three 1000-man compounds. Nearly 100 other groups of prisoners in bunch of [sic] from one to over 500 each—have shipped out by truck or train. This meant about 100,000 records sorted, typed and filed—a dozen times. This meant fingerprints, interviews, classification cards for assignment of labor. This meant counting heads in and out the gate, checking thousands of work detail passes, emptying duffel bags, searching suitcases and frisking pockets for unauthorized articles that might facilitate escape. It meant handling of incoming and outgoing mail, censoring letters and forwarding personal property of PWs. It meant decisions, discipline, and a sense of direction. It was early and late. It was work![161]

The interviews referred to in the newsletter consisted of screening the prisoners to discover if they had Nazi tendencies. Betty Dowling, the camp commander's secretary, transcribed these conversations. "Many of the prisoners seemed to be very young and older German men who had been drafted into service," she remembered. "Most were not necessarily Hitler or Nazi advocates."[162] However, interviews alone couldn't guarantee where a man's loyalty lay. That meant camp personnel needed to carefully observe the men.

With the arduous journey finally over, the German prisoners tried to adjust to their new lives. Over the next few months, they were assigned labor jobs around the camp, began to organize recreational amusements such as theatricals and also elected a camp spokesman, Karl Wanitachek (who replaced the earlier spokesman, a rabid Nazi named Rau).[163]

Labor

Since the men arrived in winter during the slow season in the agricultural world, they stayed busy with camp maintenance, working in the bakery, the hospital, the carpentry shop, the automobile repair shop and even in the camp administration building. Others did veterinarian-related tasks with the K-9 dogs (used for tracking and guarding) and army horses that were sent from Fort Robinson. Those who worked were paid eighty cents a day in canteen coupons.[164]

By May 1944, local farmers had put in requests for labor, and analysts estimated they would need around five thousand workers in the area, well above the number of prisoners available. Plans were already being made to establish branch camps in Hastings and Kearney.[165] But when harvest time came, the farmers desperately needed every man available to bring in the crops.

Like the POWs at Camp Scottsbluff, the Camp Atlanta POWs were accompanied by guards and picked up by the farmers. And also like their Scottsbluff brethren, they ended up eating food prepared by farmers' wives at the family table and conversing with the family. Relationships were made, and even after the war, many families still corresponded with former POWs in Germany.

Bill and Marge Richards were one of the first farm families to employ POWs for their ranch located near the Atlanta camp. The prisoners picked corn and helped Richards build a large pit silo. "We had to get used to the prisoners, and they had to get used to us," Richards said. He would also discuss democracy with the POWs. At one point, a prisoner who spoke fluent English told him, "But you must remember, Mr. Richards, democracy begins in the stomach." Mrs. Richards must surely have impressed those Teutonic stomachs with her cooking. "I baked cherry pies for them quite often as it was one of their favorites," she remembered.[166]

For many farm families, the prisoners became part of the family. Mrs. Bernard Modrell remembered how her son, Jim, who was eight at the time, used to ride in the back of the farm truck with the POWs. One particular incident remained imprinted in her memory. "The men were walking in from the field, and one of the POWs goose-stepping in German military marching fashion had our little boy on his shoulders," she said. "The rest of the men were singing. It was a thrill for our little boy that he still remembers to this day."[167]

Mrs. Ruby Schulz and her husband, Emil, farmed near Atlanta and used around fifteen POWs for thrashing, corn picking and shocking grain. She fed them all in her kitchen. One POW also connected with their daughter. "Our youngest girl was about six weeks old and she was lying there in her basket in the kitchen when they all came in to eat," Mrs. Schulz recalled. "He looked at her and said, 'You know, I left a baby at home about like that and I haven't heard from my wife in over a year.' It was really kind of sad."[168]

These anecdotes, as well as many others, illustrate how ideology was left behind in these shared moments. There were some things within the human experience that transcended politics and war.

Of course, other Americans besides farmers worked with POWs. Many POWs were employed in local businesses. One was the Omaha Cold Storage Plant in Holdrege, which employed approximately twenty prisoners. A former employee, Emily Scherer, remembered them as pleasant and hardworking men. "They often would sing and laugh as they worked. They were much like our own young fellows," she remembered." Scherer also believes that "ninety-nine percent" of the POWs she knew were against the war. "Another prisoner we called Cup. One day while he was at work here he received word that his family had been shot and killed. He wept openly. He had a wife and two little girls. We all felt very sorry for him."[169]

The shared humanity between American and German was further revealed when Beverly (Johnson) Carlson received a letter from a POW while working in the Post Engineers office at the camp. Though she never told anyone about it, she kept it for years, sharing it with Glenn Thompson when he wrote his history of the camp. The letter is a revealing glimpse into the life of an ordinary prisoner of war named Juergen, who was the janitor in Beverly's office.

Excuse me for writing this letter to you. I don't know why I write this. I only know that you have made someone's life easier without knowing it. You cannot imagine how hard our life is waiting day by day and week by week to just get a letter from home.

You have nobody you can talk with. Your best comrades have been shipped out to other camps and there are many other things which make you sorry. I'll tell you why I didn't run around with a bad face. When I see you, happy child-like, well dressed, and mostly laughing, I always think, "Juergen, don't hang your head. See here, not all the world is worse."

Seeing you sometimes each day makes working and living easier because for low spirits and sadness there is nothing as good as a cheerful looking maid with a lovely smile. That's it. I don't know if you can understand this because you are pretty young and never worried about anything. Now, push this letter away and say, "Oh, that little child!" Maybe, but if you understand all this, and you have too many pictures of yourself, send a smiling one to this "little child."

(Please tell nobody about this letter).

A POW[170]

Prisoner of war labor saved the harvest in Phelps County and made a huge difference in keeping the local economy running smoothly. Their help was crucial.

DAILY LIFE

Like the prisoners at Scottsbluff, the POWs at Camp Atlanta soon settled in to their new home. A cartoon by Camp Atlanta POW Alexander Wolff aptly shows this. The first panel illustrates a POW arriving in camp to a bare barracks with nothing on the shelves or on the windows. A month later, the second panel shows, the barracks has been transformed with curtains on the windows, a hanging plant, a full bookshelf and all the comforts of home.[171] While there is a slight exaggeration to this portrayal, it was accurate to say that the POWs knew they were going to be prisoners for the duration and decided to make the best of it.

One thing was for sure: the prisoners ate well. German cooks prepared the meals, working in the camp kitchen and bakery. According to an article in the Holdrege newspaper, the Germans asked to change the menu to accommodate their German tastes.

Instead of the fresh meats, there's a "bull market" with the Germans on bologna, salami and frankfurters. Cheese is all right from time to time, but tomato catsup is strictly out. So far as the Germans are concerned, you can keep most of your beets, rutabagas, turnips, fresh tomatoes, dry beans, rice,

Camp Atlanta's POW cooks hard at work. *Nebraska Prairie Museum.*

corn, hominy or sweet potatoes. But when you get down to leafy vegetables, especially cabbage and lettuce, the Germans really go to town…The POWs also consume Irish potatoes in huge quantities. They want bread, and lots of it, as well as cakes and pastries. They want fruit, but no fruit juices. The men especially hate grapefruit in any form. Tomato juice is also unthinkable to the German mind. Salted fish is preferred over any fresh meat. They prepare the softer types of fish prepared in a soup. And, of course, the Germans do eat a lot of sauerkraut.[172]

In 1945, there was some discussion that the German POWs across America ate *too* well, and in response, the U.S. government decided to reduce their rations in April 1945. Still, they weren't anywhere close to starving. The maximum caloric value for each POW was 3,400 calories.[173]

RELIGION

Worship at the POW camp was held at a combined theater and chapel outside the stockade. Religious murals painted by POW Hans Kollecker decorated the chapel walls, as did biblical quotations.[174] American chaplain Lieutenant Harry Shoal was a Lutheran and, along with three POW clergy, served both the POWs and the servicemen. Lieutenant Shoal estimated that 55 percent of the prisoners were Catholic, 40 percent were Protestant and 5 percent had no religious preference.[175] No guards were posted during services. Interestingly, during a visit in February 1944, one of the topics of concern to the POWs was the "procedure and validity" of proxy marriages.[176]

Similar to the increase in attendance at Scottsbluff religious services after the fall of Germany, attendance also increased in August 1945 at Camp Atlanta. "Besides the regular services every Sunday there are also Bible classes with altogether some fifty men attending," Sture Persson of the YMCA reported. He also noted that the Germans were grateful for the work the YMCA had done for them "in spite of the fact that the YMCA was oppressed in Germany during the Nazi years."[177]

MUSIC AND THEATER

Because the first group of POWs to arrive at Atlanta had been transferred from Camp Concordia in Kansas, there were no musicians in the bunch.

The POWs belonging to the camp theatrical group at Camp Atlanta pose for local photographer Harry Pollock. *Nebraska Prairie Museum.*

It was not uncommon for prisoners to form bands and for them to stay together during transfers. But as more POWs arrived, so, too, did prisoners who were also musicians. During his visit to the camp in February 1944, Howard Hong reported that the YMCA had provided several instruments for the camp. He also purchased an old Steinway piano that would later be delivered via army truck. He left a table model-radio-phonograph "suitable for record concerts."[178]

By July 1944, the POWs had formed a twelve-piece orchestra and were giving concerts at side camps. A year later, it was still going strong and had turned into a fifteen-piece orchestra. Sture Persson remarked, "It could easily be seen that music is an extremely valuable factor in the life of a PW camp."[179] By 1945, there were nineteen radios, one Victrola and five pianos.[180]

Unlike Camp Scottsbluff, however, theatrical performances became a popular part of life at Camp Atlanta. Thanks to a local photographer, Harry Pollock, there are several photos of the POWs in costume. It's both disconcerting and amusing to see some POWs dressed up as women, complete with wigs, dresses and makeup, to play the female roles. Shows were given in "an especially attractive and well-decorated" theater and usually lasted an hour and forty-five minutes. The shows often ran twice in one night to give every prisoner an opportunity to attend.[181]

Interestingly, a memo was sent to Colonel Smith about the possibility of paying those involved in the orchestra and theater productions. Since the men, particularly in the orchestra, practiced daily and thus did not work outside the camp, payment for their time and labor was certainly a fair consideration. This was true especially considering the impact they had on the morale of the camp. The report stated, "We benefit indirectly because anything done to divert the prisoners' minds in the right direction is to our advantage in the long run." Whether the commander eventually approved paying these performers is unknown.[182]

The theater itself was used for both the POWs and the enlisted American personnel. Because of this, the theater was perhaps more sumptuous than others around the country. The soldiers' newsletter in late 1945 stated, "Today's flag-bedecked, emerald-colored theater today with its feathered cushioned seats, rubber aisle flooring is a noticeable contrast to the hard-benched, bare-raftered auditoriums that met soldiers' eyes during the Colonel's opening talk. Colorful stage curtains, exit lights and draped windows now make the Camp Atlanta theater a rival of any."[183]

Those flags had been a source of controversy among the prisoners when they first arrived to watch a motion picture in the theater. One of the flags

A theatrical performance by the POWs at Camp Atlanta includes a POW dressed for a female role. *Nebraska Prairie Museum.*

The Camp Atlanta POW orchestra poses for local photographer Harry Pollock. *Nebraska Prairie Museum.*

on display was a Soviet flag, a current ally of the United States. The POWs "refused to return there unless the Soviet flags...were removed." However, their objections were tempered when American personnel pointed out that they "were granting them a privilege in putting the American soldiers' theater at their disposal." Presumably, the flag remained.[184]

RECREATION AND ARTS AND CRAFTS

When the camp first opened, there wasn't much in the way of recreation for the prisoners. The day room hadn't been stocked with games yet, although the prisoners took matters into their own hands and made numerous chess sets. A pool table was found for thirty dollars, and the townspeople of Holdrege gifted the prisoners with a Ping-Pong table. The local high school also donated sporting supplies, and when the weather permitted in February 1944, the prisoners played soccer and fiat ball on the athletic field.[185]

Things improved by July 1944. The prisoners had used their canteen profits to buy furniture for the recreation rooms, and there were woodworking tools and painting supplies. Colonel Smith even approved the idea of a YMCA-sponsored painting and woodcarving competition.[186] The men had their own "hobby room" where they could work on their projects. Dr. Harry Hathaway of Holdrege remembered, "Often the men made toys and presents for children of the officers and also for children of civilian families who were invited to join the officers club at the camp. They presented these to the kids at Christmas parties and so forth."[187] Many of the items the POWs made are on display at the Nebraska Prairie Museum in Holdrege.

In fact, the prisoners made most of the furniture and decorative items at the camp. "The stained glass windows in the chapel, the light fixtures and candle holders were constructed by the Germans," Glenn Thompson wrote, "as were many of the finishing touches for many other American and German buildings."[188]

Gardening was also a favorite pastime for the prisoners. Camp Atlanta had its very own Victory Garden, similar to those found in civilian areas, only much larger. Under the supervision of a local civilian, Earl C. "Peg" Carlson, the garden produced so many vegetables that the surplus was given to nearby branch camps. Vegetables grown included corn, potatoes, radishes, tomatoes, cabbages, cucumbers, turnips, carrots, onions, beans and more. The garden was so big that it required at least twenty POWs to maintain it after planting. The army brass took notice of the tremendously successful garden and gave Carlson a commendation.[189]

There was also an extensive library at the camp that included German-language books as well as English books, both fiction and nonfiction. Magazines and newspapers, from the *Omaha World-Herald* to the *Christian Science Monitor* and the *New York Times*, arrived regularly. German-language newspapers like the St. Louis *Friedenshote* and *German-American* were also available.[190] By August 1945, the camp library boasted around six thousand volumes.[191] Being allowed to read the newspapers, which didn't sugarcoat the war nearly on the scale that Nazi Germany's papers did, was a revelation to the prisoners. As Arnold Krammer noted, "The POWs continued to be amazed at the openness of the news reports, a frankness that would serve as an early part of the 'reeducation' program to follow."[192]

THE INTELLECTUAL DIVERSION PROGRAM AT CAMP ATLANTA

Perhaps the Camp Atlanta newsletter summed up the Intellectual Diversion Program best when it said, "Musical recordings, metropolitan Art Museum exhibits, radios and movies indicated to the internee that all good things are not necessarily German."[193] Through music, film and education, the IDP sought to show the German POWs at Camp Atlanta just how good democracy really was.

EDUCATION

Like other camps around the nation, Camp Atlanta offered education courses soon after the POWs' arrival. The American chaplain, Lieutenant Harry Shoaf, directed the German POW teachers, among them Heidelberg University graduate Walter Roschasch. Mathematics, bookkeeping and English were favorite topics. But perhaps surprisingly, the prisoners had taken "an unusual interest" in American history. The camp was also planning to offer a college extension course.[194] However, the courses offered changed when the Intellectual Diversion Program began.

The new assistant executive officer, First Lieutenant Dolph P. Stonehill, arrived at Camp Atlanta in December 1944 to begin implementing the reeducation program. His assistant was Corporal Martin Romain, who attended a OPMG course to prepare him for the program. Stonehill believed the Intellectual Diversion Program was critical to the future of Germany and "might help win the peace."[195]

The present POW director of studies, Walter Roschasch, was recruited to help with the reeducation program, and Lieutenant Stonehill noted that Roschasch's "influence on the program is desirable." They did not view Roschasch as having Nazi tendencies, though he and other teachers were warned that "any indication that the program is being used for political rather than educational purposes will jeopardize the entire program." From the teachers already in use, most were recruited to help in the new program, though Stonehill also had to investigate each one to check for undesirable political tendencies. If those with pro-Nazi beliefs slipped through, it could spell disaster.[196]

Remarkably, the teaching staff was paid according to how many hours of classes they taught. This was by no means a nationwide occurrence as there wasn't any specific directive from the OPMG on how or if payment should occur. Therefore, Stonehill and the Camp Atlanta staff took matters into their own hands and created a satisfactory payment system for everyone involved, one that further fueled the men's excitement for the overall education plan. Stonehill wrote, "They are all very enthusiastic about the whole plan, and have devoted a great deal of time prior to the opening of the school without payment."[197]

The education program was divided into three parts. The High School Course for Beginners was for those POWs who had finished grades five through eight (or *Volksschule* in Germany) and had started high school but never finished. In January 1945, there were forty-two men enrolled in this program, and they attended school eight hours a day, studying every subject. The second program was the Advanced High School Course. Students who had four to five years in a German secondary school (comparable to four years in an American high school plus two years of junior college) took this course and, upon completion, would be ready to take an examination for a university. Forty-five men filled this course and also studied eight hours a day on all subjects including English, math, history, Latin and biology. The final program, Night School, offered business and university-level courses, as well as general interest and trade subjects. Attendance wasn't mandatory, and often, the PWs in this option worked during the day. Courses offered included advertising, shorthand, history of art, bookkeeping, French and even music theory.[198]

For those PWs participating in these schools who wished to earn credit, the German government "provided a printed enrollment book, in which a student has a running record of his educational progress, signed by his teachers. When these prisoners return to Germany, they will thus receive credit for the work done here." Stonehill requested a supply of these booklets from the International Red Cross.[199] Later, an Administration School was added for those German soldiers who qualified through their years of military service to enter the German equivalent of the American Civil Service. This program prepared the soldiers for the examination they had to take to be in the Civil Service. All subjects were taught, and the students attended only four hours a day.[200]

University courses hadn't yet been offered but were in the works. Professor K.O. Broady from the University of Nebraska visited the camp on January 18, 1945. Stonehill met with Broady to see about establishing correspondence courses, loaning films and books to the POW camp and having German-speaking lecturers come to the camp.[201]

Unfortunately, a hiccup occurred. There was, as Major Paul Neuland put it, "a lack of cooperation on the part of the University of Nebraska," which was "noteworthy."[202] Stonehill received a letter from Broady that stated they would be unable to provide the camp with the necessary reference books or any other further material because "those titles which might be available are in storage. We are planning to move to a new and much larger library at the close of the war and when we do some books will be available. Of course, it will be too late then to help the POW Camp at Atlanta."[203]

This letter was forwarded to the Education Branch and eventually landed on the desk of Major Maxwell McKnight, the director of the POW Special War Projects Division. In a memo dated April 9, 1945, McKnight stated:

> *The lack of cooperation on the part of the sponsoring university resulted from an initial impression of the representative that the universities [sic] participation in the educational program of the camp would be confined to the furnishing of reference books and training material. The University of Nebraska has recently been authorized by this division to present approved correspondence courses to Prisoners of War at Atlanta. The granting of authority to provide correspondence courses will encourage the University of Nebraska to make available its facilities for the development of the educational program at the camp.[204]*

Whether or not the University of Nebraska eventually cooperated with the program at Atlanta isn't clear. Available records indicate that Lieutenant

Stonehill continued to ask for lecturers from the University of Nebraska, and these requests were sent to the OPMG for approval. One in particular, Professor William K. Pfeiler of the University of Nebraska–Lincoln, was thought to be a great choice to speak to the German POWs on the inner workings of democracy. His knowledge was desperately needed. After Germany surrendered, Lieutenant Stonehill wrote a May 1945 memo to the OPMG office.

> *It is the opinion of the undersigned that the time is ripe for more direct methods…the PW educational leaders at this camp have already "indoctrinated" themselves on democratic ideas and now openly seek more information. They report a significant fact—that the PWs are now in a confused state of mind and that something must be done to set them thinking in a straight line. They report that many of the staunch Nazis are shifting their thinking to extreme Communism as an alternative to Nazism.*[205]

Animals were kept as camp mascots or pets in many POW camps. Here, German POWs at Camp Atlanta pose with a cute puppy. Notice the PW letters on one of the prisoners' pants. *Nebraska Prairie Museum.*

It is not clear if Professor Pfeiler ever made the trip to Camp Atlanta nor is it known if those POWs who turned to Communism ever had their thinking "set straight."

While Lieutenant Stonehill continued to appeal to the University of Nebraska, another problem arose. It appeared that not many POWs at Camp Atlanta *wanted* to take university correspondence courses. Many of the men were not at the university learning level, and the fact that they had to complete their courses using the English language was a further detriment. In addition, those who didn't work couldn't afford the tuition, while those who *did* work were too tired by the end of the day to attend class.[206]

To address the problem of learning English, Lieutenant Stonehill ordered records from the Linguaphone Institute of New York. The learning method of the Linguaphone Institute (a company still in business today) was simply to "Listen, learn, speak." Students listened to records, read as they listened and only after they understood what they were saying were they encouraged to speak. In March 1945, there were approximately 172 prisoners enrolled in Linguaphone classes.[207]

In only a few short months, the enrollment of men in classes went from 460 to 891, largely due to Lieutenant Stonehill's efforts. Major Paul Neuland wrote of Stonehill, "His frankness with the prisoners of war and clean-cut personality assures the future success of the Intellectual Diversion Program."[208]

Der Ruf and the Atlanta Echo

The reception of the nationwide POW camp newspaper, *Der Ruf*, wasn't an immediate success at Camp Atlanta. The Germans in compound two recognized it as propaganda (though why this particular compound was singled out in the report is a mystery), but as more copies arrived, more men began to read it. It cost five cents and was issued on a semimonthly basis. POWs could contribute to this newspaper, but at Camp Atlanta, some worried there would "be a reaction against them if they did so."[209]

However, by March 1945, the POWs and Stonehill prepared a "dummy copy" of a new camp newspaper they called *Atlanta Echo*. The newsletter would not contain military or political news but camp news only. "With careful censorship," Major Neuland reported, "and stimulated interest in book reviews, film reviews, sport review, cartoons, and branch camp news, it should prove to be a good publication." Issued semimonthly and costing five cents, the paper was a success. However, by July 1945, the "nonpolitical" tone of the newspaper changed, ostensibly due to the Allied victory in Europe. The July issue contained quotes from Thomas Mann's *Achtung Europe*, articles about the history of America and the Fourth of July and an editorial by one POW, who wrote, "We will not put our head into the sand, but decisively break with the past and start from a new point believing in a future of security, freedom, and self-determination."[210] The American soldiers' newsletter even commented on these editorials, stating that they "provoke thought."[211]

MOTION PICTURES

As early as May 1944, the POWs at Camp Atlanta were able to watch films twice a week. Admission was fifteen cents in canteen coupons. Unfortunately, at this point, the American personnel at the camp couldn't choose what films to watch but had to settle for whatever the film circuit managers sent. Because this was before the Intellectual Diversion Program came into effect, these films were not censored. Sometimes, according to reports, many of those films would "offer uncomplimentary pictures of the Nazis and of their leader, Hitler," which would undoubtedly not please the prisoners.[212] Special Services and Theater Officer Lieutenant Friedman was in charge of censoring these films and, according to Major Neuland's report in early 1945, "had made an excellent beginning" in the Intellectual Diversion Program before Stonehill's arrival.[213]

When Captain Lakes visited the camp in February 1945, he noted how much the German POWs enjoyed watching films and newsreels from the Army-Navy Screen Magazine. Directed by Frank Capra, this film program was produced biweekly by the United States Army Signal Corps' Army Pictorial Service for members of the U.S. Armed Forces. It contained newsreels from around the world, cartoons, variety shows by current entertainers and feature stories from the American homefront. One film shown to the POWs, a film about General Clark decorating Japanese American soldiers in the Fifth Army (undoubtedly the famed 442nd Infantry Regimental Combat Team made up entirely of Japanese Americans), sparked the POWs interest. In the film, General Clark commented that America was "made up of all nationalities." The POWs also watched a film about how Americans voted on election day as well as one portraying the sacrifice of an American fighter pilot battling a Japanese carrier. Lieutenant Stonehill and Lieutenant Friedman both agreed that the Army-Navy Screen Magazine films needed to be included in the film circuit since "the prisoners of war request these specifically, and are more prone to believe such films as truth."[214]

Lieutenant Stonehill believed in the program's necessity. "We're not trying to 'make Americans' out of Germans, but we present 'America' so they'll go home with a 'healthy respect' for it."[215]

CAMP ATLANTA POLL ON THE INTELLECTUAL DIVERSION PROGRAM

Looking at modern Germany today, with its parliamentary, representative democratic government, it might be easy to conclude that the American-held POWs who returned to Germany put their democratic knowledge to good use, thus validating the reeducation program. However, there is no hard data to make this a definitive conclusion. We do, however, have a few clues.

In December 1945, a large cross-section of German POWs was polled by the Office of the Provost Marshal General before they were repatriated: 22,153 men from Camp Shanks, New York, who represented all nine service commands and were polled before embarking on ships back to Germany; prisoners attending a special democracy school at Fort Eustis, Virginia; and prisoners at Camp Atlanta. Camp Atlanta was chosen because of Lieutenant Stonehill's well-known, outstanding work on the reeducation program. In many other camps, the reeducation program was only halfheartedly administered.

Almost all militant Nazis had been weeded out of these groups and sent to other camps earlier in the war. The men were asked their opinions on everything from, "Were the Jews responsible for the war?" to "What is the most important single idea you have learned during your internment in America?" The results were sometimes surprising. For example, when the men from Camp Shanks were asked, "Do you believe that Jews were the cause of Germany's troubles?", the answers indicated that the Nazi propaganda had indeed run deep. Of the men, 33 percent answered "no," 49 percent answered "partly" and 8 percent answered "entirely." Another 10 percent declined to answer. In their analysis, the OPMG determined, "The comparative failure to re-educate the prisoners with respect to race prejudice runs parallel to the experience of our own nation, which has discovered that this is the most difficult of the undemocratic attitudes to dispel."[216]

A more disturbing result came when all three groups were asked, "You have seen moving pictures and a booklet concerning concentration camps in Germany. Do you believe that such conditions did exist—or do you think it was just some false propaganda we dreamed up?" The results were as follows:

	Fort Eustis	Camp Atlanta	Camp Shanks
True	94 percent	68 percent	36 percent
Propaganda	2 percent	14 percent	32 percent
No answer	4 percent	18 percent	32 percent

At Camp Shanks, there were 22,153 PWs polled. OPMG analysis concluded that at Camp Shanks "the disappointing percentage of prisoners (36 percent) believing the concentration camp films to be true may have resulted in part from a guilt complex."[217] While this is certainly possible, it is more telling that so many did not answer the question. War guilt over the Holocaust continues to be a huge issue in modern-day Germany. Incredibly, Holocaust denial still exists to this day despite overwhelming evidence to the contrary.

However, Camp Atlanta's answers throughout the poll are indicative of the success of the reeducation program, thanks to the direction of Lieutenant Stonehill.

AFTER THE WAR

All branch camps under Camp Atlanta were deactivated in December 1945. Camp Atlanta itself was deactivated in January 1946. By that spring, the last POWs boarded a train and left Atlanta. In the upcoming months, camp buildings were sold off. Some were bought by civilians and put to use, while others were deconstructed and used for materials. All that is left of the camp today are a few concrete foundations, a water tower and a tall brick chimney from the heating plant. Otherwise, the physical camp is gone.[218]

Many former POWs kept in touch with friends they had made in America, whether by working for them on their farms or in the camp itself. Some, after returning to Germany and finding the conditions dire, wrote to American friends and asked for help. Hubert Halfmann found his village and home destroyed and his family starving. Halfmann wrote to the Nebraska farm family he'd worked for during his stay as a German POW at Atlanta and

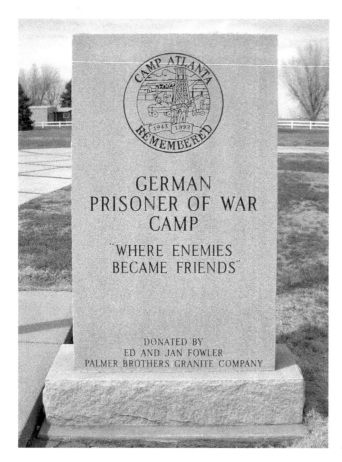

A monument outside the Nebraska Prairie Museum pays tribute to Camp Atlanta, "Where Enemies Became Friends." *Author photo.*

told them of his hardships. The family responded with food care packages. In 2005, Halfmann said that his family would not have survived without that family's generosity.[219]

Another prisoner, Rudolf Ebers of Hamburg, Germany, wrote a letter to Camp Atlanta's Protestant minister and appealed for help in November 1947.

> *I have lost everything during the big air raids of 1943 on Hamburg. We have nine children, one of them still missing…Prospects for the coming winter are as bad as never before and I do not know how to bring my family thru this terrible winter of hunger and sadness. For this reason I am addressing you this letter and beg you, for God's sake, to hand this letter over to some party or member of your church who is willing to help a poor family in Germany.*

The community responded. The Atlanta Women's Society sent packages of "food, winter coats, shoes, thread, elastic, and other sewing items." Ebers was incredibly grateful and kept corresponding with the women. Eventually, with their help and the help of the McGinley family in Ogallala, two of Ebers's children were able to immigrate to America.[220]

There were, of course, those German POWs who decided to return to Nebraska in later years. One was Otto Schwinzfier, who had worked for Myatt Volentine's car dealership in McCook, Nebraska. Volentine sponsored Schwinzfier so he could immigrate to Nebraska. "He worked for me for two or three years in McCook," Volentine later remembered. "Otto was a master electrician in Germany so he was able to do any kind of electrical and tune-up work on automobiles."[221]

In October 1993, the village of Atlanta held a "Camp Atlanta Remembered" reunion. Several former POWs attended.

Overall, the POW experience at Camp Atlanta had been a positive one, giving many German POWs an excellent taste of American democracy and kindness.

CHAPTER 5
FORT ROBINSON POW CAMP

Fort Robinson has been a steadfast fixture on the Plains of northwest Nebraska for more than 130 years. Located seventy-five miles north of Scottsbluff and twenty-two miles west of Chadron, the fort is situated in the heart of an escarpment that suddenly shifts from rolling plains to tall, pine-covered buttes. This area is part of the Pine Ridge.

After America entered World War II, Fort Robinson became an ideal location for the K-9 Dogs for Defense program. The dogs were used mostly for sentry and guard duty at defense plants and military installations (including, as was previously mentioned, POW camps like Camp Atlanta). In 1942, Fort Robinson began to implement plans to host a training center for the dogs, complete with 150 handler-trainees and ninety-six kennels. New buildings were also constructed for the program, consisting of a veterinary building, classroom and training buildings and a conditioning and isolation building. By October 1944, Fort Robinson "was the nation's leading dog training center, with 3,565 dogs having been trained and issued, and 1,353 dogs on hand."[222]

The fort's role would expand once more with the coming of thousands of German prisoners of war. It was isolated, it had excellent railroad connections and the work projects for the prisoners were numerous. Since it was an army remount depot, housing thousands of horses as well as K-9 dog units, prisoners would find no shortage of things to do. All in all, the fort seemed a perfect place for German prisoners to wait out the war.[223]

This historical sign and a few concrete foundations mark the location of the Fort Robinson POW Camp. *Author photo*.

The camp itself was located about a mile and a half from the military base. It was activated on May 1943, and after further construction to enlarge the camp (completed that fall), it had the capacity to hold three thousand men.

AMERICAN AND POW PERSONNEL

Two companies, the 331st and 635th, of the Military Police Escort Guard (MPEG) were stationed at the camp. Camp administration consisted of the 1765th Service Unit. They served in camp headquarters and as intelligence staff. Others also were cooks, chauffeurs, interpreters and clerks.[224]

Except for brief stints by Lieutenant Colonel Lester Vocke and Colonel Jay E. Gillfillan, Colonel Arthur C. Blain served as commander of the Fort

Robinson POW Camp. Howard Hong described him as "courteous and rugged."[225] The intelligence and supply officer was Lieutenant Clarence L. Duell, and Captain Jason R. Silverman was the assistant executive officer. Sergeant Alfred Thompson later served as assistant executive officer and headed the Intellectual Diversion Program.

The newly elected POW camp spokesman was Stabsfeldwebel Harry Huenmoerder. The PW camp translator, Unteroffizier (Sergeant) Wolfgang Dorschel, a "progressive non-Nazi NCO," replaced Huenmoerder, a pro-Nazi, in early 1945.[226]

THE GERMANS ARRIVE

The first German prisoners to arrive at Fort Robinson came from the North Africa campaign. The division consisted of members from Rommel's Tenth Panzer Division and had different units from around Germany. Stuttgart was its base. The division had fought in Poland, and in 1941, it was in the central part of the Russian front. In 1942, badly crippled from fighting, the division was sent to France to refit. These soldiers were transferred to Tunisia in late 1942 and were captured in May 1943.[227] After traveling through the United States via trains from Virginia ports such as Northampton, they arrived at Fort Robinson on November 19, 1943.

Former prisoner Otto Ludwig remembered years later his first impression of the fort. "When I was a young boy, I had a lot [of] books about Indians, living in America, and I heard about the prairies, the mountains, all these things. But my first impression has been when I arrived in Fort Robinson this is a very lonely place. And I am a prisoner of war."[228] Another former prisoner, Wolfgang Loesche, said, "The imprisonment that I encountered in Africa on the part of French, English and America was altogether different from that which I found at Fort Robinson. And here in Fort Robinson, after the few days when so to speak, I had a foothold, I did not experience any difficulties."[229]

Like other German soldiers, Karl Deyhle had already formed impressions of the Americans thanks to German propaganda. But that changed when he was captured:

When we were captured we saw that the Americans had thousands of tanks which was [sic] stored right in the open air for the supplies of the needs of the American machineries. Thousands of dollars of gasoline. This tremendous overpowering might on the side of the Allies, so impressed me, that I thought that the whole war had become senseless...One believed on the basis of the news that came from Germany that in the Atlantic there were no more Allied ships because of the U-Boat threats. And of course, this was not the case. Instead, on our passage to the United States, we saw hundreds, convoys of hundreds of ships. We could not count them all...Naturally, this impressed me tremendously, as a young person, to see that contrast between what I saw and what I thought was the case of the basis of the news I had heard earlier.[230]

Years later, Deyhle described how he sent letters home to his family, asking them not to send him any packages, as he had more than enough at Fort Robinson. He also said that when he wrote of positive things about the POW camp, German censors struck them out.[231] His favorable impressions of Fort Robinson were shared among many of his comrades.

LABOR

There was no shortage of labor for the PWs at Fort Robinson. Many prisoners took advantage of the opportunity to work on the nearby post. In compliance with the Geneva Convention, they were paid at the rate of eighty cents a day, the same as the base pay of a private. At Fort Robinson, Class I labor included maintenance and administrative work in the POW camp itself. Class II labor was used at the fort and POWs engaged in "post Engineer and Quartermaster activities such as loading and unloading lumber, working in the fuel yard, hauling gravel, cleaning horse traps, working on feed bunkers, hauling manure, working in the dairy barn, working on picket line and handling rations." Class II work projects also centered on the remount station and dog training station, which offered labor for approximately one thousand prisoners.[232] Other jobs included working at the veterinary section of the post. By 1945, reports stated that since the thirty prisoners had begun working in the veterinary section, "German PW labor made it possible for the unit to continue to function."[233]

A memo was circulated to U.S. Army personnel at the fort with directions on how to treat the prisoners. Such instructions included, "Do not try to gain information from Prisoners of War," "Do not ever believe a Prisoner of War likes you; he does not," "Do not think a PW will not escape if he can. He will" and "Do not talk to PW's except in the line of duty."[234] In January 1945, around seven hundred prisoners were employed at the fort. "Many of them are taking the place of soldiers and civilians in specialized jobs which include running the Post Bakery, certain skilled labor jobs and the care and maintenance of large numbers of animals," according to a memo from the director of Service Installations Division. "The relief of these trained men at this time would work a considerable hardship on the Post at Fort Robinson."[235]

This was typical of camps located at military installations. They needed POW labor to free up U.S. servicemen for other war-related duties. Nonmilitary installation camps and branch camps often had the task of organizing labor for public and private contracts. Prisoners from camps such as Scottsbluff and Atlanta had a far greater impact on the agricultural needs of the local communities than did prisoners from Fort Robinson.

In fact, only a small fraction of POWs at Fort Robinson worked in agriculture. In mid-1944, farmers in the small community of Whitney, some fourteen miles northeast of Fort Robinson, were finally granted the use of POWs to help with planting, cultivating and harvesting crops. The only problem the camp administration faced was how to furnish the necessary guards. A signed contract was sent to the Seventh Service Command in Omaha for approval, but whether it was ever approved is unclear.[236]

Working with the war dogs was a favorite for some of the POWs, and it showed in their work. Major Don L. Mace from the Chemical Warfare Service, Edgewood Arsenal, Maryland, came to visit the fort in March 1945 to test gas masks on the dogs, horses and mules. He was pleased with the care given to the dogs. "This kennel area was being maintained with a very minimum of (U.S.) personnel," he reported. "Practically all of the labor was being done by some sixty Prisoners of War. Dogs, in general, were in excellent condition and receiving the best of veterinary care and supervision."[237]

Of course, not all POWs were eager to work. Some of them either outright refused or caused mischief while on the job. PW Rodolf Fleischfresser was one such laborer. "He is argumentative when assigned to duties," Roscoe J. Craig, the fencing foreman, wrote in his report asking Fleischfresser to be removed from his detail, "and attempts sabotage in the manner of throwing nails in the path of vehicles, turns on the switch of the vehicle and at one time grabbed the gear shift when I was trying to drive."[238]

Two German POWs, Private Alfons Hartung and Sergeant Alfred Hoedl, were confined to quarters for "failure to obey order of German non-commissioned officer to go to work" and "hiding out from work." The Geneva Convention actually permitted this type of confinement under Articles 54–59. How long the men were confined is not clear.[239]

In a rather disturbing note, before Colonel Blain took command of the camp, those who went to work at the nearby fort were not checked for contraband when they returned to the POW camp. Blain soon learned of this "oversight" and ordered a general shakedown. Charles Eberhardt was shocked at what turned up. "An almost unbelievable number of improvised knives, nippers and other articles made from metal was found and confiscated." Despite the POWs' objection to being searched, this convinced Eberhardt that Colonel Blain was "entirely in the right" to have instigated the search, and from then on, all POWs were searched whenever they left or entered the POW camp.[240]

After the war ended, fort-related labor eased, and other farmers were granted the use of prisoner labor from Fort Robinson. Former prisoners remembered how the farmers and their families chose to break the rules in dealing with prisoners, just like farmers and their families did with prisoners from Camp Scottsbluff and Camp Atlanta. Elmer Raben, a farmer who lived north of Crawford, enlisted the help of prisoners to pick 170 acres of corn. Lunch was provided by the camp and consisted of a slice of salami and bread. But Raben refused to allow the men to work on such light fare. Instead, Mrs. Raben always prepared chicken and noodles or stew in addition to their meal.[241]

There is no question that the PWs working at the Fort Robinson post made a noted difference in keeping the fort running and freed up American personnel for vital war-related jobs.

DAILY LIFE: RELIGION

Protestant and Catholic services were offered for the German POWs. The camp chapel could hold 250 men, though it was rare to have anywhere close to that amount at services. Protestant church services were held every Sunday at 10:00 a.m. with regular attendance from 60 to 80 men. The camp contained two Protestant POW ministers—one Lutheran, the other Calvinist. For the Catholics, Father Albel of Crawford was assigned to the post, but a prisoner of war priest, a Benedictine from Münsterschwarzach Abbot in Germany, held the church services. Sunday services were held at

9:00 a.m. and had an attendance of between 80 and 90 men. Both groups also held Bible study classes.[242]

Howard Hong said the U.S. authorities attributed the camp's two Protestant ministers with "keeping up the tone of the camp" simply by being available to talk to the men, conducting services and Bible studies and through their earnest desire to make a difference. "The two prisoner pastors are personable men and realize that of all the men in the camp they alone are able to follow their professional life-calling," Hong reported.[243]

Interestingly enough, Huenmoerder, the POW spokesman, didn't count the pastors or their work as an achievement worth mentioning: "The judgment of the spokesman was that the best achievements in the camp have been the school, then sport, then theater and music, and finally films." Hong reported six months later in January 1945: "Significantly, he did not mention the religious services and the pastor work of the PW clergy. Others in the camp, both Americans and PW's, would place the religious interest and work on a par with the excellent educational program."[244]

Huenmoerder's Nazi leanings undoubtedly colored his views of the pastors and religion itself. However, six months later, Huenmoerder was no longer the spokesman. The new spokesman, Wolfgang Dorschel, attended religious services, so there is every reason to believe he appreciated the clergy much more than his predecessor.

Like Camp Scottsbluff and Camp Atlanta, after Germany lost the war, attendance at religious services increased substantially. Carl Gustaf Almquist wrote, "Church attendance in this camp is very high, the highest I have heard of, with almost 48 percent of the whole camp attending services." The two pastors also took their responsibility to take Germany out of the ashes of defeat quite seriously. In discussions with Almquist, one pastor insisted that "total separation of church and state" was the only solution for Germany to move forward while the other took a radically different direction, wanting Christianity to infuse government with Christian thought and become a powerful entity in the state. Regardless, both men thought the key to change was in educating the youth. "They were intelligent and fine men," Almquist stated, "in whose hearts was a living faith and an entering into the spiritual life of Christianity with its possibilities for building a new world, since all has failed in their own country."[245]

After the war, Dorschel told a story of how he first met the local Catholic priest, Father Albel. "The second day in the camp a civilian priest came up [to] the camp...I remember that the guard at the gate mentioned, 'Father, be careful they are damned Nazis and they might kill you.' So I told the guard and of course Father Albel in English that we were soldiers and he could enter the camp without losing one hair except for the wind."[246] The two went on to have a solid friendship built on mutual respect.

MUSIC AND THEATER

At the Fort Robinson POW Camp, the PWs had a thriving theatrical and musical community. As early as December 1943, shortly after they arrived, they were already enjoying performances by the Forty-seventh Regiment of African Grenadiers band. Except for three members, this forty-piece German regimental band had all been transferred to the camp along with their instruments. One official visitor reported that the band "gives magnificent concerts" and said that the camp commander knew "the influence music has on the morale of the prisoners."[247] Unfortunately, the band didn't stay long after an incident in early summer 1944. Apparently, the band was giving a regular weekly concert, which included refreshments. The prisoners, however, only appeared interested in the food and not the music, staying long enough to grab a bite to eat before leaving. Charles Eberhardt noted in his report, "The musicians, as true *prima donnas*, resented this attitude and asked to be transferred to a larger camp." Their wish was granted, and they were sent to Concordia, Kansas, on June 14, 1944.[248]

Thankfully, there were other musicians in the camp, and even in late 1944, a fifteen-piece dance orchestra was organized. This group would go on to support the theater program and assist with performances.

The theater program was incredibly popular. The PWs named their theater company Varista. According to assistant executive officer Alfred Thompson, this was a contraction for *Variete im Stacheldraht* (Variety in Barbed Wire).[249] Beginning in January 1944, the Varista group started building a stage for its performances in one of the barracks. The group presented "variety-type" performances and didn't delve into more serious matter. "There is little interest on the part of the theater group for good drama," Howard Hong noted in July 1944.[250] This theory is born out when looking at pictures of the theater productions. They often depict men dressed up as women in hilarious caricature-like costumes.

But the theater company sank its teeth into something a little more substantial in January 1945 when it presented two acts from *Die Fledermaus*, a popular German comic opera by Johann Strauss II. The same performance also included eleven variety acts consisting of juggling, music and comedy.

Since the Varista Hall, as it came to be known, could only hold 160, these shows were shown as many as eighteen times so all the men in the camp could attend. But with the help of a professional entertainer, POW Willi Schwind; an orchestra; and a PW tailor who helped make costumes, the shows were surprisingly well done considering what the PWs had to work with.[251]

Later, music would also become an important part of the Intellectual Diversion Program as the PMG sought to bring new melodies to the PWs. A list was sent out of "approved" musical selections, and the Special Project Division stated, "It is not the purpose of this list to restrict or censor recordings played in the camps. The idea is rather one of variety, to enable prisoners of war to hear music of other countries, to impress them with the fact that music is universal and not national, and to show them the high standards of orchestras and artists." The list included German, Italian, English, French, Russian and American composers. The most famous of German composers made the list—Bach, Beethoven, Brahms, Handel, Mozart, Schubert, Strauss and even Hitler's favorite, Wagner. American composers included George Gershwin, Stephen Foster, Jerome Kern and Richard Rodgers of "Rogers and Hammerstein" fame.[252]

RECREATION AND ARTS AND CRAFTS

Soccer was the most popular sport at Fort Robinson for the German POWs. More than forty years later, former PW Karl Deyle fondly remembered winning the compound soccer championship. "Under the circumstances, I lived and we lived well," he recalled.[253] By January 1944, the camp had already organized nine soccer teams even though the fields had yet to be finished due to snow on the ground.[254] But thanks to the wide-open spaces of the Nebraska prairie, the prisoners would have a space of 1,600 by 500 feet, which, according to the Swiss representative, "will afford ample space for several soccer fields."[255]

The mild winter of January 1945 saw the POWs playing "almost continuous" soccer games. In fact, they had so many games that Howard Hong reported that they had to start a referee class "in order to have enough arbiters for all the games going on. Thirty-two men are in the course under

This ship was built by a prisoner of war at Fort Robinson and is indicative of the truly remarkable artistry among the men. *Author photo.*

the leadership of the sports director, a professional referee."[256] Clearly, the Germans took their soccer playing quite seriously.

Soccer, of course, wasn't the only sport they played. Track and field, boxing and handball were also popular. One report calculated that nearly two thousand POWs were active in some sporting event, and that was likely a reason for "the robust and healthy appearance of so many of the men."[257] Other activities included cards, chess and checkers, the latter two often used in tournaments.

As in other camps, U.S. personnel set up a workshop within the stockade for making furniture and doing woodworking. This workshop included hand and power tools. Luis Hortal reported that this carpentry shop was "the pride of both prisoners and American authorities alike." Carpenters could earn fifty cents a day working there.[258] Painting, woodcarving and sketching were also popular pastimes. Some of these handmade objects are on display at the Fort Robinson Museum today.

MOTION PICTURES

Watching films was not an option for the prisoners who arrived in late 1943. However, profits from the camp's canteen could be used to purchase a sixteen-millimeter film projector, and by January 1944, the sales were high enough to buy one. POW Wolfgang Dorschel mentioned Marlene Dietrich's costume classic *The Flame of New Orleans* in his diary entry in February 1944. "Wonderful!" Dorschel wrote. "Still the old Marlene as 1930 in the *Blue Angel*."[259]

The movie house at Fort Robinson consisted of two barrack buildings. Once every five days each prisoner could attend a film program that consisted of a feature-length film and two shorts. To pay for the rental of films, $100 was withdrawn from the POW fund every ten days. The intelligence officer at the time, Captain Silverman, and the camp spokesman usually wrote a short synopsis of the film to distribute to those prisoners who lacked English skills.[260]

Strict regulations of films did not exist before the reeducation program. Up until 1945, movies were usually selected by the camp spokesman, Harry Huenmoerder. He made it a point to select movies that "showed American life in the worst possible light."[261] Howard Hong noted this, as well. His report of July 31, 1944, said that although there was no shortage of men at the movie house, "they did not especially care for most of the films." Hong reported that "the low quality of content left upon them a deepening impression of an inferior America that there is nothing other than whiskey, drinking, gangsters, wild women, and horse thieves." Worse, Hong said that the prisoners had been overheard discussing the films. "'If this is America,' they have heard said, 'America is a century behind us.'"[262]

In his letter of February 13, 1945, Sergeant Alfred Thompson shared his perception of the camp spokesmen's film choice. "They purchased from private companies the worst of movies one could choose, interspersed with musicals and heavy drama which appealed to the extremes. Deanna Durbin ruled the roost, with Tex Ritter and his pals on the other side of the corral fence. America became to them a land of half-naked women, fighting families, the roaring West, and the gangster East."[263] Dorschel's diary is testament to both Thompson's assessment and Howard Hong's report. Movies listed in his diary included numerous Abbott and Costello's films such as *Ride 'em Cowboy*, which Dorschel called "very, very funny"; *Hit the Ice*; *One Night in the Tropics*; *Pardon My Serong*; and *Who Done It*, which Dorschel called "nice, a funny criminal film."[264]

But Thompson suggested another reason as to why only certain films were available to the prisoners. He stated that many private companies were out to

Films starring Hollywood darling Deanna Durbin were wildly popular with the Axis POWs in Nebraska and throughout the country. *Wikimedia Commons.*

make money by selling cheap films to the camps at a "fat profit." Thompson wrote, "They filled their shelves with trash, advertised a half hundred of good films of which they had but a few copies, and sluffed (*sic*) the bad films off on the PW camps as substitutes."[265]

But not all of the films selected before the implementation of the film program were of detrimental value. Supporting evidence is found in Dorschel's diary. His January 5, 1945 entry read, "*As You Like It* from Shakespeare as film with Elisabeth Bergner as Rosalind, in Old English and [I] read the American text. A very good film." January 21, 1945, read, "A film about settler[s] and their towns in America. The war with Indians. And the revolution war 1775 was good." [266]

With the advent of the Intellectual Diversion Program, films shown to the POWs came under much closer scrutiny and in fact, became a critical role in the program itself.[267]

THE CAMP'S FINAL DAYS

The PW population at the camp dropped to 2,100 in February 1945 when Fort Robinson became a camp for German enlisted sailors. Nearly all German army PWs were moved to other camps in the Seventh Service Command except for a few hundred of the first men to arrive in December 1943. Because of their work ethic, they were retained.[268]

After Germany lost the war, the Nazi salute and all references to Nazi symbolism (flags, insignia, posters, etc.) were banned. It was also mandatory for all POWs to watch the Nazi atrocity films on the concentration camps.

The Special War Projects Division decided that the atrocity films could be used as a lesson in "collective guilt," as well as a tool of reeducation. The prisoners at Fort Robinson were aware of the films before they arrived. "As yet we have no news of Atrocity Films, but expect to have them in [a] short while," Thompson wrote in June 1945. "Most of the internees await with anxiety their arrival and showing. News that other camps have already had opportunity of seeing them disturbs them no end, for they fear they shall be left out of the program."[269]

The films arrived a month later on July 31, 1945. Wolfgang Dorschel wrote, "Showing a film from a *Konzentrationlager*. The film made a deep impression on the PWs."[270] But the Nazi ideology had run deep as some prisoners refused to believe the evidence in front of them, convinced the bodies of the Jews killed by the Nazis were, in actuality, India natives killed by the British in India.[271]

The army decided to gradually deactivate the POW camp in September 1945, and it became a branch camp of the Scottsbluff POW camp. The last prisoners left in May 1946. Due to the lumber shortage, it didn't take long for the camp buildings to disappear, and many of them were sold. Only one warehouse remained by late fall.[272]

Today, all that remains of the POW camp is a stretch of prairie dotted with concrete foundations flanked by name markers where the former buildings once stood. A section of the Fort Robinson Museum, part of the Nebraska State Historical Society, is dedicated to the POW camp. Of interest is an *Afrika Korps* uniform worn

The uniform worn by Dietrich Kohl, a German POW at Fort Robinson who served in the *Afrika Korps*. *Author photo.*

by German prisoner Dietrich Kohl at the time of his capture, which he donated to the museum in 1996, as well as examples of arts and crafts made by the prisoners, such as ships in a bottle and artwork.

After World War II, Fort Robinson's original use as an army remount depot came to an end. Today, it is a Nebraska State Park and is a very popular tourist destination.

For many of the German POWs held at the fort, the experience in America was one of the best of the war. Years after they left the United States, they returned to the site of their captivity, this time as free men. Wolfgang Dorschel visited the fort a total of three times until his ailing health made it impossible to return. He maintained contact with the curator of the Fort Robinson museum as well as other comrades.

Dorschel returned for his last visit in 1991 with former German POW Dietrich Kohl. Although they were at the camp at the same time, they did not meet until 1987. "With so many men in the compound, it was impossible to know everyone," Kohl said. Dorschel reported that he had been in contact with around twenty-five other ex-POWs and said, "We are friends, and we will be friends until we die." After Dorschel returned to Germany, he worked for the American military administration in Munich as a result of his participation in the democracy seminars at Fort Eustis and eventually ended up in the liquor export and import business in Frankfurt.[273]

Other former prisoners who returned for reunions included Alois Siegmund, a painting contractor who settled in Rushville, approximately fifty miles east of Fort Robinson. Siegmund immigrated to the United States in the 1950s, returning to work with a former army sergeant at the camp, Ed Sydow of Rushville. Siegmund had worked for Sydow at the camp's bakery, and Sydow was unable to find help for his own bakery after the war. Sydow wrote to Siegmund, asking him to come to the United States to work for him. By the time Siegmund arrived, Sydow had sold the bakery, but Siegmund stayed and started his own painting business. "I never regretted becoming an American citizen," Siegmund said.[274]

All the returning POWs had nothing but positive memories of Fort Robinson. Of course, it must be stated that time has a way of distorting one's memory. But much of their memories are in keeping with current records of the time, and all indications point to their experience at Fort Robinson being a positive one. Although this is only a fraction of the men who were imprisoned at the camp, it is still worth noting their reactions to their confinement years later.

PART III

CASE STUDY:
A CLOSER LOOK AT THE INTELLECTUAL
DIVERSION PROGRAM AT FORT ROBINSON

CHAPTER 6

NAZISM AND REEDUCATION AT FORT ROBINSON

It took a few months after the prisoners arrived for the staff at the Fort Robinson camp to implement a full educational program. With no inkling that the government would undertake a reeducation effort in the months to come, two intelligence officers decided to start their own "school."

Alfred Thompson had come to the camp as a private and an interpreter with the Intelligence Office, having taught high school German in North Dakota before the war. He and fellow intelligence officer Dr. John C. McGalliard of the University of Iowa taught English to around sixty prisoners each by the end of 1943. "It was tough going," Thompson later wrote. "We had no materials with which to work. All that we did have to work with had to be censored each time we entered and left the gate. Even blank sheets of paper had to bear the mark of the censor or we couldn't get it past the sentries." Thompson expressed frustration at not being able to take his teaching material into the compound "because it was not approved by official mark of the censor."[275]

The difficulties did not end with the censors. It was hard to keep students, let alone find those willing to take the courses, simply because they thought they would be punished for allowing themselves to be surrounded by "foreign indoctrination." Thompson reported that many POWs told him of the threats they'd received for taking the English courses. Even more disturbing was the prisoners' assertion that the Nazis had "spies in the class whose only purpose for being there was to control the discussion and prohibit expression of opinion."[276] Yet the school continued to thrive until the need for assistant instructors became necessary. Since American personnel fluent in German were scarce, Thompson turned to those German prisoners fluent in English, such as Wolfgang Dorschel.

Encouraged by the prisoners' reception to the classes, Thompson took the program one step further, and the two intelligence officers decided to begin their own educational program with two purposes in mind. First, Thompson wished to keep the prisoners from dwelling too much on the fascism that still ruled behind barbed wire, even though they were thousands of miles from Germany. Second, he hoped to gain a "toehold" on the inner organization of the camp in order to control activities of the Nazi group.[277]

Thompson's vision pushed the program into a new direction, and more classes on various subjects, from engineering to music, were added. For a time, the only textbooks available for use were the "battered English volumes and a great number of 'Studienblaetter' sent by the International Red Cross, printed by the German Army for use in the field, just as the American army had done for its men. Most of this publication was not bad, but some of it carried subtle Nazi propaganda which the censors did not catch in first readings."[278]

According to Luis Hortal's report on January 21–23, 1944, Thompson had been keeping busy. Three classes of "English Beginners" existed at the camp with a total of seventy-five students. One "English Advanced" class was attended by seven POWs. Other courses had been planned and would gradually go into effect. These classes included American history and geography; basic architecture with drafting, carpentry, masonry, plumbing and locksmithing; several musical education classes; and a few religion classes. The instructors wished to begin a course on economics, but again, they ran into difficulties as the commanding officer "was not very keen on this subject as it might be a source of controversy."[279]

Those in charge of the prisoner camps were often the ones who opposed the education program at this early stage. According to Thompson, "The inside operation of the camps was to most camp administrations a closed and unopenable book. A common expression was, 'We know of and are interested in only that portion of the PW day which is between "count" in the morning and "count" in the evening: what takes place at night is not of interest to us.'"[280]

This attitude was further evidenced at Fort Robinson after the commanding officer changed from Colonel Gillfillen to Colonel Arthur C. Blain in February 1944. The educational program suffered a blow when Thompson and McGalliard were ordered to "cease indoctrination." Thompson admitted they had failed to follow the rule in the camp operations directive

The old grave-digger (of the Empire) is getting suspicious

*"What are those two grinning about?
Do they think this grave is for me?"*

Front of a German propaganda leaflet featuring caricatures of Churchill, Stalin and Roosevelt. The reeducation program sought to eradicate this type of propaganda from the German mind. *Ed Reep Collection. Courtesy of Susan Reep.*

MOSCOW
and
WASHINGTON

have already decided
the fate of Great-Britain

They want to reduce her to an unimportant "Red Island" on the fringe of a (hoped for) Soviet-Europe.

Uncle Sam takes Britain's riches, her gold, her money aud her foreign investments under the clever Jewish "lease-lend" scheme. U. S. troops are in India and nearly 20 other British possessions, naval bases and zones of interest. The Far-East has been lost to Japan.

Communist Stalin takes the rest, starting with Iran, Iraq, North Africa, Finland, Rumania, Bulgaria, even southern Italy and Egypt. His agents are everywhere, undermining British influence, British prestige.

AI - 107 - 9 - 44

Back of a German propaganda leaflet declares the U.S.'s lend-lease agreement with Great Britain to be a "Jewish scheme." *Ed Reep Collection. Courtesy of Susan Reep.*

that "prohibited the discussion of political issues with PWs. This was an order from high headquarters based upon the provisions of the Geneva Rules. But, fact of the matter is, we did not discuss political matters except upon request of the Prisoner of War, and then, only in secrecy." One intelligence officer ordered Thompson to burn his card file of PWs, telling Thompson, "We have no interest in the political opinions of Prisoners of War; we are interested only in peace and quiet inside the fence. The anti-Nazis are worse than the Nazis."[281]

This only points to the strong grip of Nazism in the camp. Camps with pro-Nazi spokesmen offered a well-run camp of discipline and order, the very things a camp commander wished to have. Political discussions would only disrupt the "peace and quiet" of camp life.

Even though Thompson's original intentions for the educational programs remained intact, his venue for seeing them suffered for a time, along with student attendance. Unfortunately, Thompson's supervisory role was limited. Even though the school gradually gained interest again, Thompson no longer had control over the curriculum, thus making it "impossible to control the effect of the program."[282]

Wolfgang Dorschel was one of the prisoners who attended classes. Elected camp translator on January 28, 1944, Dorschel took a keen interest in the education program, and his avid interest in America and democracy stemmed from several factors. Unlike his father, Dorschel refused to join the National Socialist Party, even when he was drafted into the German army.[283] It is not surprising, then, that Dorschel eagerly worked with the American personnel on the education program.

Even though many prisoners spent their days toiling under the hot Nebraska sun during the summer, battling what Dorschel called "a very big heat and no breeze," the prisoners continued their education.[284] Howard Hong even remarked on the prisoners' resilience: "In spite of the work program and the prairie heat, dust, and wind of the summer, the school continues." In the summer of 1944, the education program had grown. Classes were composed of three classes of English, two of French, one of Italian and one each of German language and literature, German history, general science, mathematics, higher math, chemistry and physics, *Bau Schule* (Construction School), *Ingenieur Schule*, (Engineering School) and interior design. All classes were held in the evening, with the exception of *Bau Schule* and *Ingenieur Schule*, which were held in the morning.[285]

A year later in January 1945, Hong again visited Fort Robinson, reporting that the "best achievements" in the camp included the education program.

Hong discovered that around two thousand men were participating in classes, a remarkable number considering Thompson had started with around sixty prisoners in his English courses. Five divisions now existed: architectural design and building, high school, spot high school courses, college level and other spot courses of college level and technical level. Plans were even in the works for translating textbooks, such as *Thermodynamics*.[286]

The Intellectual Diversion Program officially became implemented in the camps following the receipt of a memo dated November 9, 1944. In the first of many memos to the commanding generals and officers of POW camps from Brigadier General Robert H. Dunlop regarding the reeducation program, it detailed the program's purpose, aims and goals. Specific instructions were given to United States personnel. "Its success, however, relies on the clear recognition by all United States personnel who have contact with or control over the prisoners that it is not a program of palliative entertainment, but a highly important undertaking which is to receive active rather than passive support on all possible occasions by all concerned."[287]

Thompson noted the marked contrast of the memo to the previous concerns regarding education: "Where formerly there was discouragement for the school program, suddenly the camps were overwhelmed with encouragement for all types of educational activity."[288]

By February 1945, Thompson mentioned the reeducation program, albeit not directly, in a letter to his brother, Rob, who was stationed in the Pacific Theater. "I now have a new job with the Recreation and Education office under the Assistant Executive Officer," he wrote. "We, however, handle both the Prisoners of War and the Americans in the program…The past week we embarked upon an education program which is unequalled in any camp in the territory…It is our desire to bring the educational opportunity to all the men at this station including the Germans. If things pan out as we hope to have them, we should be making history at this station."[289]

The attitude of camp personnel toward reeducation at Fort Robinson underwent a dramatic reversal with the receipt of this memo. In other camps throughout America, though, the attitude of American personnel toward the prisoners was not favorable, even with the presence of a memo from the OPMG. There was strong anti-German sentiment prevalent among Americans and even POW camp personnel.

Yet such was not the case at Fort Robinson or, indeed, at any of the other Nebraska camps. Anti-German sentiment was not evident. In fact, it is difficult to find much evidence of prejudice against the German prisoners from the areas surrounding the camp. Neither does Alfred Thompson mention any anti-German sentiment in his detailed letters. It may well be that this could largely be attributed to the substantial German immigrant settlements throughout Nebraska.

With this lack of anti-German sentiment at Fort Robinson, reeducation was not received with as much cynicism as elsewhere. Thompson was overjoyed at the newfound attention to what he had considered a "Renaissance of learning" for the prisoners, believing that he and his fellow teachers had been "pioneers" in the program who "broke out in exuberance at the thought that our ideas had finally found root somewhere."[290]

Fort Robinson was a leading camp in the education effort. Thompson praised the camp's contribution to the reeducation program and stated, "We are engaged in the biggest educational program of any camp of this sort in the country." Well over two thousand men were enrolled in the program by February 1945, and courses were offered from intermediate grades through college level with some of the latter being carried out through the American University program for both prisoners and American soldiers. Thompson thought it rather remarkable that both captor and captive could avail themselves of an education: "It is strange to think of German Prisoners of War taking the same courses from the same universities as do the men who are their captors, their guardians, this is the case at this camp."[291]

Thompson also believed wholeheartedly in the principles behind the reeducation effort: "Thus far we have had absolutely no trouble, have done an immense amount of good in making these Prisoners of War feel that America and Americans are not so bad." Thompson also made reference to how he felt the government originally planned to administer the POW camps.

> At the outset it was not the express purpose of the government to run PW camps in this way, but they have since changed their minds. After all, it is in the interest of the future world that these men return to their homes with a feeling of good will and respect rather than the alternative. We may accomplish much in this direction of employment of the proper policy here. What can happen in the other direction may be seen by looking at some of the other PW camps over the United States; they are not all as well handled as is this one.[292]

Thompson attended the screening-orientation conference at Fort Slocum, New York, in May 1945. Since the program was still classified as "secret," Thompson and the rest of the candidates who attended had no knowledge of what awaited them. But like many of the other officers who finished the ten-day conference, Thompson was eager to return to Nebraska and apply his knowledge of the Intellectual Diversion Program to the camp at Fort Robinson. But upon his return, he found some of his ideas strangled by the realities of army administration. "You cannot know the discouragement one feels when he finds his worthy ideas, the product of a great deal of thought, buried beneath the cold negation of a two letter word from the top-seat," he wrote in a scathing letter to his parents dated July 7, 1945. Thompson believed the men in charge of the program were unfit to implement it: "Above the men who speak the German language, know the German mind, understand the previous German political ideology and interest themselves in the course of German Prisoner of War reeducation, have been placed an assembly of ignorance which is the anathema of the ideal for which we fought, for which we now strive, and towards which the peace must be directed." Thompson lamented the loss of the enthusiasm on the part of intelligence officers across the country who longed to return to the camps and implement their ideas, only to be cruelly disheartened.[293] But even though Thompson suffered setbacks on his quest to fulfill the IDP, he persevered and continued to push its importance.

Some American lack of enthusiasm for the reeducation program was also noted by Dorschel, although he does not specifically mention Fort Robinson. Instead, he mentions Camp Scottsbluff in his entry of October 28, 1945, in which he says, "A co-worker came by and told us that Scotts Bluff is not the Ideal camp. It has 40% Nazis, 30% communists and 40% more or less anti-Nazis. In that camp is the old German Wehrmacht commando!... It is known in all sidecamps that an old Wehrmacht's guy or one young man from the HJ [Hitler Jugend] is a camp spokesman. Very little interest from the American side to retrain the POW in their way of thinking like Wehrmacht and Nazi-Germany. Now they [are] wanting to make a fast program, which we had here more than 6 months ago."[294] This only points out the difference between those who desired to make a difference in the prisoners' reeducation and those who did not. The enthusiasm with which Thompson and Dorschel viewed the Intellectual Diversion Program spoke of their belief not only that it was needed but also that German prisoners would greatly benefit from participating.

Thompson's contemptuous view of the way the Intellectual Diversion Program was implemented did not echo into the secret documents passed to the assistant executive officers by the OPMG. They wanted to make it perfectly clear that the program was not one of government indoctrination but instead encouraged "self-indoctrination" to those prisoners who might prove "susceptible to its influence." The office specifically said that the program did not "contemplate any attempt to Americanize them."[295] However, the push to incorporate all things "American" in the classroom became evident. Thompson wrote of the publications available for a very low price in the POW canteen. Known as the "Jones Manuals," they included books on the American government, American history, music in America and the American educational system.[296]

With the realization of the reeducation program, detailed documents were sent to the assistant executive officers describing the books to be used in the classroom, library and canteen. In a memo of November 10, 1944, a book list was included with the following categories: fiction and drama (general and American); anthologies; history of art, literature and music; history; biography; politics (general and American); travel; philosophy; and psychology.[297]

With the focus of the reeducation program centered on the English language and the teaching of American history and democracy, many of the more technical classes were threatened. Thompson lamented the repeated focus of these two subjects, convinced that the Germans would not need knowledge of history and English when they returned to Germany after the war, but "an education which can break the back of poverty and ruin which rides slipshod over the German nation today." In his letter of June 30, 1945, Thompson eloquently stated the issue he felt the American government faced with the POWs. "We may convince the Germans that America is the greatest nation in the world today—that they already believe—but if we fail to put them and their peoples back on the road to recovery, if we cannot put food in their stomachs, clothes on their backs and roofs over their heads, our glorification of the American ideal will avail us little."

But Thompson also believed in the prisoners' earnest desire to leave the old school of thought behind. "These men want to help themselves, ask only for the opportunity of putting their homeland, their lives in order. The nation or the political philosophy which can first do that will win their confidence and support."[298]

Winning such confidence and support was greatly helped by an organization the prisoners at Fort Robinson began on their own. *Arbeitsgemeinschaft zur Pflege der Politischen Aufklärung* (Working Association for Political Enlightenment) began with a group of twenty prisoners, nearly all progressive anti-Nazis, who for months met secretly in order to lay the groundwork for their democratic program. To belong to the society, an oath had to be taken—a permanent and unconditional break with National Socialism. By the end of July 1945, over 90 percent of the prisoners at Fort Robinson had joined and had signed a contract to break with Nazism. Even though the organizers purposely wanted to make the organization "exclusive" to those whose politics were less than desirable, Alfred Thompson reported that those who did not belong to it desired to be let in so much so that in the end, "we finally had to admit them all."[299]

The foundation of the *Arbeitsgemeinschaft* was the lectures and discussions that packed the lecture halls to the point of the camp personnel's scrambling to find space for those in attendance. The group's goal was "the reeducation and stabilization of all misguided persons in their midst."[300] Thompson rejoiced at the attendance of the POWs, noting, "The lecture halls were filled to overflowing with men who for the first time in fifteen years dared to speak their minds." But it was the freedom of speech Thompson enthusiastically shared. They were able to "discuss freely the future of Germany, to reveal her past, to decry her leaders, to declare themselves ready to repair the damage the Hitler mob had wrought upon the earth and her peoples."[301]

Dorschel, a progressive anti-Nazi, was a founding member of *Arbeitsgemeinschaft*. Harry Huenmoerder, who was ousted as camp spokesman in mid-1945, had been sent to Camp Clark, Missouri, where, according to Thompson, "all good Nazis go." Dorschel was appointed camp spokesman for the remainder of the camp's existence. Thompson felt Huenmoerder's dismissal was an asset to the reeducation program. "It has meant the difference of success and failure in the program," Thompson stated. "[S]ince we have a new spokesman, we have arrived at a point where we may consider the mission well in hand." With an anti-Nazi spokesman in charge of the prisoners, reeducation had a fighting chance at Fort Robinson.[302]

In conjunction with the lectures of the *Arbeitsgemeinschaft*, the classroom also was a vital tool to reeducation. It is worth taking a closer look at the classroom by examining a lesson plan put out by the OPMG. A model American history course was sent to the assistant executive officers on June 25, 1945. Because of their translation into German, Allen Nevins and Henry S. Commager's 1942 work, *The Pocket History of the United States,* and J.T. Adams's 1931 book, *The Epic of America,* largely formed the base of the course. The packet included an outline of eleven lessons, suggestions of training aids, a short paragraph on how discussions should be led, a bibliography and a final examination consisting of fifty true and false questions.

The Provost Marshal General's Office considered the teaching of American history to the prisoners as one of the reorientation program's primary aims. In accordance with such thinking, the lesson plans rarely, if ever, touched on negative portrayals of the United States. However, instructors were also told that during the discussion period, the instructor should "make no attempt to whitewash American history, but should of course avoid being maneuvered into a discussion of topics not included in the scope of this course. He will best disarm hostility and at the same time impress on prisoners our fairness of mind, if he says frankly that everything has not always been perfect in America." The document further encouraged instructors to divert undesirable questions by pointing the POWs to further readings on the subject.[303]

Of course, American history textbooks did not portray the entire truth. Columbus's slaughter of thousands of Native Americans is not mentioned in the volumes of the 1930s and 1940s or, indeed, for many years after. According to Frances FitzGerald, textbooks of the 1940s portrayed imperialism as a European affair. They concentrated on the Monroe Doctrine and the Good Neighbor Policy, using words like "we" and "our" in order that students could identify with the lessons.[304] Even though many textbooks emphasized America's isolationism, the Special Projects Division banned Charles and Mary Beard's *Basic History of the United States* (1944) for the "latent isolationism" found within the Beards' "economic interpretation of America's involvement in international power politics, as well as the book's consistent portrayal of idealism and principles as nothing more than a rationalization of economic and political considerations." Historian Ron Robin concurs with FitzGerald's assessment and argues that the historiography of postwar America "portrayed America as a country unafflicted by the social cleavages of the Old World."

Even though there were varying interpretations of American history available, the Special Projects Division picked those that would best serve its purpose. The officers in charge of the literature division of the Special Projects Division devised a reading list that focused on the "unifying dimensions" of America instead of the divisions permeating American history.[305] Taking their philosophy one step further, the Special Projects Division actually wrote their own versions of approved literature by heavily editing questionable material. A series of "ideologically correct" books was the *Buecherreihe Neue Welt* (New World Bookshelf) published by the OPMG and was available only in the canteens of POW camps.[306] According to the Special Projects letter dated February 21, 1945, the assistant executive officers of each camp were to stress two important facts to the prisoners: "the books are published at the request of the prisoners and are new cheap editions of books hitherto unavailable or published at prohibitive cost."[307] A list was included with the letter of forthcoming books in the series. Such books included American Wendell Willkie's *One World* since it showed that American isolationism was gone, and thus, there was no hope for further German aggression. Franz Werfel's *Die Vierzig Tage des Musa Dagh* was a novel of "resistance of a suppressed people against the brutal methods of their conqueror" and featured a German as its "most positive character."[308]

However, in an earlier memo regarding the arrival of these books, the Special Projects Division stated, "The fact that sale of these German books is being promoted by the War Department and that their procurement and distribution in any way differs from that of other canteen supplies will not be disclosed to prisoners and will not be published in any manner." The books were cheap—twenty-five cents a copy. In addition, the books were not to be placed in the camp libraries until their sale in the canteen had been "actively promoted."[309] In general, the books that the New World series published attempted to accomplish varying degrees of reeducation. William Saroyan's *Human Comedy* attempted to emphasize "branding any one person, nation, or ethic group as 'bad.'" Reviving an Austrian sense of identity was represented by such books as Joseph Roth's *Radetzkymarsch* and the Franz Werfel books. Karl Zuckmayer's *Der Hauptmann von Köpoenick* (The Captain of Köpencik) sought to "slaughter the sacred cow of German militarism."

It also did not escape notice that Zuckmayer was an exile from Germany who lived in California. Another aspect of the series was the disproportionate number of Jewish authors, such as Franz Werfel and Arnold Zweig. Erich Marie Remarque's *All Quiet on the Western Front* was chosen "for its objective account of the horrors of war" and also because it had been very popular in Germany but had been "viciously attacked by the Nazis ever since its publication." Other German authors were chosen for their "impeccable anti-Nazism." Many were exiles and had given positive reviews of the United States, thus endearing them to the Special Divisions Project leaders.[310]

If sales figures were any indication of the success of the series, then business was good at most camps. However, sales figures alone did not show the whole picture. Boredom, a constant enemy of the prisoner, might have accounted for many of the sales, as many were desperate to read anything available in the German language. As repatriation to Germany drew closer, the books' low prices also led many prisoners to purchase them as souvenirs of their stay in America. Still other radical German loyalists sought to remove the books as quickly as possible to undermine the reading program.[311]

Other references in the American history lesson plan also focused on the positives of American history and included some very direct statements. One such statement was listed in the colonization section: "The colonization of America involved people from different countries and of various religious beliefs. They learned to live harmoniously in the same land."[312] No mention is made of the "harmony" between the Native Americans and colonists, but it does emphasize the diversity of America and the American attempt to incorporate people of varying beliefs, religious and otherwise, into one cohesive nation. Such statements were not only indicative of the American educational system at the time but also stressed the differences between America and Germany. Another lesson stated, "These qualities, which sum up Americanism, were already to be found in the colonial period: mixture of many nationalities, religious toleration, individual opportunity, independence of the individual, energy and optimism," and religious toleration was further stressed with the following statement, "Many religious faiths worshipped side by side—Catholics, Protestants, Jews."[313]

The lesson plan on the era of the American Revolution was perhaps the most involved. Essential points of the Declaration of Independence were listed, such as "All men are created equal" and "People have the right to abolish their government, but not for 'light and transient reasons.'"[314] These were key ideas of democracy, even though racial segregation and slavery were part of society when the founding fathers drafted the Declaration and the Constitution. But the Special Projects Division did not emphasize those negative aspects, just as the American educational system did not. Yet such democratic ideals remained powerful tools to introduce German prisoners to democracy.

The most telling statement of the American history course was included in the final lesson entitled "America in the 20th Century." In the introduction of the class, the instructor was urged to say the following: "Today we shall discuss the direction in which American life has been moving during the last decades, and attempt to show you that America still is what Lincoln said, so many years ago, 'the last best hope of earth.'"[315] This neatly summarized the Office of the Provost Marshal General's attempt to showcase America on the best possible terms. Unfortunately, it also failed to emphasize the second-class citizenship of African Americans.

But what the Special Projects Division taught in the prisoner of war classroom was not so very different than what was being taught in the typical American high school classroom. Textbooks of the early 1940s focused on "the glory of free enterprise—they were far more enthusiastic about it than the Bill of Rights," and the word "capitalism" was never used.[316]

Of course, it is possible that controversial topics did come up for discussion in the classroom. These textbooks were available in German to use for the class, and there are no indications that they had been censored. What is clear, however, is that the topic of American intolerance was not directly woven into the fabric of the lesson plan. The average German prisoner might have read and noticed the statements regarding intolerance, but it is also probable that their own skewed versions of racial intolerance, a product of Nazism and the society of Hitler's Germany, led them to believe nothing was amiss in such statements.

Nazi indoctrination must be considered in the reeducation program. The average German prisoner held captive in the United States "was not a fanatical ideologue. He was a nationalist...and in large measure wholly captivated by the mystique and omnipotence of Hitler's leadership." Some prisoners had been professional soldiers, while others were wartime conscripts. The varying circumstances of their capture also impacted their views. When a survey was undertaken in the beginning stages of the reeducation program, "approximately 40 percent of the prisoners could be considered pro-Nazis (between 8–10 percent were judged to be fanatic, and about 30 percent were deeply sympathetic)." But of even greater significance was the survey's indication that "confidence in Adolf Hitler was not synonymous with an attraction to National Socialism; nor did blind obedience to military orders and tradition indicate a sympathy for Nazism."[317]

However, the first captives captured in North Africa, which included the first prisoners to come to Fort Robinson, "were the most thoroughly indoctrinated Nazis."[318] This makes the presence of the *Arbeitsgemeinschaft* at Fort Robinson all the more significant. But it does point to the difference between those soldiers who did not subscribe to Nazism, such as Wolfgang Dorschel, and those who did, such as the ousted Nazi camp spokesman, Harry Huenmoerder. When the grip of Nazism within the camp walls was broken, it enabled those anti-Nazi and more progressive soldiers to explore other means of political expression.

Those who were open to the new democratic ideals relished the opportunity to learn about America. Dorschel took a trip to Fort Meade, South Dakota, with Captain Silverman for a meeting regarding the reeducation program. On the way to Fort Meade, he passed one of America's most recognizable national monuments, Mount Rushmore. He noted in his diary on June 20, 1945, "And now we (are) coming to Rushmore memorial, where Lincoln, Theodore Roosevelt, Jefferson, and Washington was carved into the natural stone mountains. The head of Washington is 60 feet high. For me a shrine of democracy."[319]

Was the Intellectual Diversion Program a Success?

Alfred Thompson reflected on the reeducation efforts at Fort Robinson while he was at the special democracy seminars at Fort Eustis, Virginia. His thoughts on the program offer an appropriate and appreciative glance into the minds of those who believed wholeheartedly in their mission:

> *I feel that I have won a great battle, that I have proved myself capable of beating a task which I often times thought was impossible to whip…It has not been a fight in which the laurels gained at the end are pinned on one's chest, nor is it a fight in which one gains a bank roll. It is a fight to prove the worth of man, to prove that there is an intrinsic inborn God-given worth to every person, and that even the demoniac teachings of a Hitler cannot destroy that worth; and that if one practices what he preaches he can regain that which others claim has been lost for all time.*[320]

It is hard not to believe that the IDP at Fort Robinson did not make some sort of impact on the prisoners. The presence of *Arbeitsgemeinschaft* alone is evidence that the time and energy of those American personnel and progressive German soldiers dedicated to introducing democracy to the average POW was not in vain.

Wolfgang Dorschel was one who truly believed in democratic ideals, and he was determined to share his knowledge with others in order to help create a new Germany. If only one man carried the concepts of the Intellectual Diversion Program with him to Germany and continued to believe in their importance, then the reeducation effort was a success. But without the enthusiasm of American personnel, such as Alfred Thompson at Fort Robinson and Lieutenant Stonehill at Camp Atlanta, the prisoners at Fort Robinson and Atlanta would not have achieved the amount of reeducation that they did.

Thompson and Dorschel epitomized the IDP's ideals. Though they began the war as enemies, a friendship was created through their dedication to the reeducation program, one that lasted long after the war ended.

Since the United States government failed to do a follow-up study on the reeducation program years after the last POW made his way back to Germany, valuable data was lost. Studies on various camps around the United States do little to unearth information regarding the IDP except to briefly mention it in passing.

Such conclusions will take much more research and study, if such is even possible with the World War II generation on both sides of the Atlantic fast disappearing. The success of the government's "experiment in democracy" remains unfathomable. While historians can do their best to piece together the remnants left of the camps or track down still-surviving POWs in order to do a study on how the reeducation program affected their lives, such studies will take time and tenacity. But for the intrepid scholar, it is time well spent in order to unearth the success of one of America's largest secrets during the war.

PART IV

THE BRANCH CAMPS

It is very difficult to find information on the individual branch camps. Since they were not located near military installations and reported directly to the main branch camp, documents and records often fell through the cracks. Most of the branch camps were placed at already existing sites near towns. For example, the branch camp at Bridgeport was located at the fairgrounds about a mile south of town. This was typical of most branch camps throughout the United States.

Branch camps functioned the same as main camps. Most of the men held here were expressly used as local labor. The International Red Cross and the YMCA also visited these camps, though finding these reports is difficult. As you will see, there is more information available on some camps than on others.

Fort Robinson's only branch camps were located in South Dakota.

Note: Branch camps not located in Nebraska will not be profiled here.

CHAPTER 7

CAMP SCOTTSBLUFF BRANCH CAMPS

C amp Scottsbluff had five known branch camps in Nebraska. They included Bridgeport, Bayard, Lyman, Mitchell and Sidney. There were also camps in Veteran and Torrington, Wyoming.

To help educate the local populace about the purpose and logistics of the branch camps that would be near the Mitchell and Lyman communities, Lieutenant Colonel Dempster from the Scottsbluff camp spoke at a Rotary meeting in Morrill, Nebraska, on March 16, 1945. (Morrill was a good halfway point in which to hold the meeting since it was located between Mitchell and Lyman.) He explained the "general requirements under which the prisoners could be employed" and how the contracting process worked.

The insignia of Camp Scottsbluff featured Scotts Bluff National Monument. *Legacy of the Plains Museum.*

Colonel Dempster explained the new "piece-work" arrangement in place for POW labor. This mean that a "minimum amount of work is required of a prisoner of war to earn the specified daily wage in canteen coupons." The more work the POWs did, the more canteen coupons they could earn.[321]

Bridgeport

Bridgeport is located about thirty-five miles west of Scottsbluff in Morrill County. The *Bridgeport News Blade* reported on June 7, 1945, that approximately two hundred prisoners of war had arrived at the camp located at the fairgrounds south of Bridgeport. First Lieutenant Donald A. Edwards, along with twenty enlisted men, came from Camp Scottsbluff to run the camp. County agent E.C. Nelson said that most of the POWs would be available for farm labor. The POWs were much in demand. Nelson said that almost all those farmers who didn't have their own labor supply had contracted with the camp for POW labor.

Two buildings were used out at the fairgrounds. The stock barn, used as the mess hall, was divided in two to accommodate the soldiers and the POWs. Enlisted men slept in the poultry building. POWs were housed five to a tent. A large fence had been erected around the camp along with floodlights.

The POWs supplied their own cooks, and their menu was fairly simple. Oatmeal, milk and bread for breakfast; a sausage sandwich and perhaps bean stew for lunch; and mixed peas and beans, potatoes, coffee and bread for dinner. The article was quick to point out that "there is certainly no evidence of 'coddling,'" though the writer also didn't hesitate to note that the POW diet was approximately 2,500 calories, "twice that allowed the people of Holland under German occupation."

The POWs mostly worked in the beet fields:

> *Each prisoner doing beet labor is required to complete one-quarter of an acre of blocking and thinning per day and they stay in the fields until the task is complete. They work in details of ten to 12 men, each with a military guard. They do not work on Sunday unless an emergency arises and then the work is voluntary. The prisoners are paid at the rate of 80 cents per day, which is paid to them in canteen checks which they spend at their own post exchange.*[322]

Donna Blome Amateis of Bridgeport remembers her father sending her brothers to the fairgrounds to pick up German POWs to work on their farm, the Camp Clark Ranch, every morning during the summer. "Six or eight of them would come out and hoe weeds in the corn and the beets and alfalfa," she said. Both her parents were fluent in German and spoke often to the POWs. "When Mother looked in their sacks and saw the sorry-looking sandwiches they had, she knew she had to cook for them," Amateis remembers. Since the Germans were not supposed to eat in the house, they took the stock tank and turned it over to use as a table. Her mother cooked them the old German dishes, like *kuchen*, and also fixed homemade chicken and noodles. "They were the nicest, most polite men you'd ever meet," Amateis said. "They were very courteous. They called my sister and I *Frauleins* and called my mom *Frau*. They always said, '*Danke Schone.*'"[323]

Darlene Hoffman Cowden grew up on a farm between Bridgeport and Bayard. During potato harvest, her father, Otto Hoffman, used POW labor from Bridgeport. Cowden remembers working in the fields with the POWs. "I drove the farm truck in the fields while POWs picked up the filled potato sacks, [and] sat them on the truck while the POWs on the truck stacked them in a way so they would not fall over," she wrote.[324]

Donna Cranmore remembers walking out to the POW camp after school in the evening. "The sun would be low and the camp stood out plainly, with the rocks [Courthouse and Jail Rock] beyond," she wrote. "There were many tents in neat rows. There were many prisoners and guards, they were always getting supper and setting up camp for the night." Cranmore also worked in the potato fields with the POWs along with other students, although an "imaginary line" divided the prisoners and the teenagers.[325]

The Bridgeport newspaper reported a prisoner escape on July 12, 1945. Two German POWs, Theodore Rogge and Otto Koch, were working in a field near Bridgeport when they "just walked away." The two were found near Fort Morgan, Colorado, and returned to the Scottsbluff POW camp.[326]

BAYARD

Records on this branch camp are quite scarce. On June 2, 1945, the *Star-Herald* reported that a branch camp housing 181 POWs at Bayard, located in Morrill County approximately twenty-three miles from Scottsbluff, had been established. According to a brief article in the *Bayard Transcript* on July 12,

1945, those who wished to hire POW laborers for hoeing beets or beans or to do other farm work were to see Mr. Burnham at the Farm Bureau Office in Bayard.[327] The prisoners were housed at Great Western Sugar Factory's dormitory in Bayard. Today, this building is the House of Transfiguration.

MITCHELL

As early as March 1945, the Great Western Sugar Company's abandoned dormitory had been proposed as a location for a branch camp in the small farming community of Mitchell. Located approximately twelve miles from Camp Scottsbluff, the camp was in operation by June 6, 1945. The extensive preparations to the old building were done "quietly" and housed 213 prisoners. The camp also included a large compound for exercise. A high wire fence was built completely around the camp with men "walking post" in front. There were twenty-five American officers and men assigned to the Mitchell camp.

Farm labor associate Harry Amen said the POWs were available for labor in the surrounding area. Not surprisingly, the *Morrill Mail* noted, "Those in charge are anxious to keep the prisoners at Mitchell busy."

By October 18, the POWs had been working in the beet fields in the Mitchell area. The beet crop was about 65 percent harvested by November 8. County agent Wesley M. Antes said that with more POW labor, it should take only about ten days to finish the harvest. He was right. By November 15, the harvest was not only finished, but POWs were also "piling tops and bean threshing."

With the end of the harvest came the end of the branch camp. The last of the German POWs at Mitchell were sent to Douglas, Wyoming, around December 13, 1945. The *Mitchell Index* noted, "Farmers using the prisoners here the past season express considerable satisfaction with their work…[it's] generally agreed that without this labor, this year's crops could not have been produced." It appeared, though, that there were those who weren't anxious to see the prisoners leave: "Men in touch with the situation said it is more advisable to keep the PWs here for work than to import Mexican nationals or Jamaicans." Since the Scottsbluff camp still had prisoners, people could still apply for labor there.[328]

LYMAN

Controversy surrounded the placement of the POW camp in Lyman. Located about twenty-five miles from Scottsbluff, the village was scheduled for a labor camp. But the American Legion resisted the POWs' being housed in the business section of town, though it did not object to a place outside the city limits. The Legion sent a resolution to the *Lyman Leader* on March 15, 1945, that said placing the camp within city limits would "be debasing the Morals of a free people" and that law and order could not be maintained if a resident was "slurred or scandilized (*sic*) by lurid scenes or actions." The community held a meeting (attended by 150 people) and formed a committee to study the problem. They soon found a solution. A tent city camp was built west of the Great Western Sugar Factory. In addition to tents, the camp consisted of a large mess hall moved from the Guernsey (Wyoming) CCC camp. The *Lyman Leader* reported, "The personnel will be housed in tents upon concrete floor, with 8 for the enlisted men and 61 for prisoners." The 300 POWs arrived at the end of May 1945 and worked for local farmers until they were sent back to the Scottsbluff camp on November 29, 1945.[329]

SIDNEY

In Cheyenne County, the Sidney branch camp was located ten miles northwest of the town at the Sioux Ordnance Depot. The name was later changed to the Sidney Army Depot. The army established it in May 1942, and its sole mission was "the receipt, storage, and issue of all types of ammunition from small arms to 10,000 pound bombs, all types of general supplies from small automobile parts to jeeps, and various strategic and critical materials." The depot was on 19,771 acres of land and employed a large number of civilians as well as army personnel.[330]

In May 1944, approximately six hundred prisoners, half of them Italian and half of them German, were sent to the depot. Temporary barracks were erected as well as a barbed-wire stockade. An Italian Service Unit, the Seventieth Italian Quartermaster Service Company, was formed on May 1, 1944. Those men could officially do work for the war effort, and many of them worked at the depot itself. They could move freely around the depot, but they couldn't go into Sidney unless they were part of a group with an accompanying officer. They did, however, attend church in Sidney at St.

Patrick's and even formed the Sioux Italian Choir. Singing was a favorite pastime among the Italians, and they also gave a public concert at Band Shell Park in Sidney.

The Germans at the Sidney branch camp worked hard, mostly laboring in the fields, but local citizens described their attitude as aloof. Still, both the Italians and Germans enjoyed playing soccer, attending movies and doing other extracurricular activities the same as those at other POW camps.

One Italian POW, Emanuelle Campanella, who was captured in North Africa in 1943, was first sent to Camp Scottsbluff before arriving at the Sidney camp. After the war, he returned to Italy and then arranged to come back to America. He married a girl from Sterling, Colorado, and owned the Cedar Creek Garage between Sterling and Sidney.[331]

CHAPTER 8

CAMP ATLANTA BRANCH CAMPS

Atlanta had more branch camps than did Scottsbluff and Fort Robinson. They were not all operational at once, but all were active between 1944 and 1945. They included Grand Island, Hastings, Kearney, Franklin, Hebron, Weeping Water, Elwood, Bertrand, Alma, Lexington, Palisade, Ogallala, Benkelman, Hayes Center and Indianola. There were also two in Kansas: Hays and Cawker City.

ALMA

Alma is located twenty-five miles south of Atlanta in Harlan County. Here, on November 14, 1944, approximately 115 German POWs lived in an abandoned but comfortable school building that contained a kitchen and a large dining hall decorated with proverbs and landscapes by the POWs. Some POWs were employed with the local poultry food-processing plant, though most had first harvested corn and worked on farm repairs.

The Germans enjoyed playing football on the football field outside and had been paid a visit from the Camp Atlanta orchestra. Though the assistant executive officer for the Intellectual Diversion Program, Lieutenant Stonehill, had only been to the branch camp once since becoming AEO, he wanted to implement the reeducation program at Alma. Books were rotated between Alma and Atlanta, and a complete listing of all the books in the

Camp Atlanta library were provided to the POWs. Lieutenant Stonehill planned to transfer a qualified instructor from Atlanta to help with the education program and intended to start evening classes.

During his inspection, Major Neuland stressed a need for more German-American dictionaries and recommended that a number of newspapers and magazines needed to be available for the men. The POWs were especially interested in the German translation of the *Omaha World-Herald*.[332]

INDIANOLA

In a strange twist of fate, Indianola had actually started as a base camp in the summer of 1943. Located in Red Willow County, the small town of Indianola is a little over fifty miles from Atlanta. The camp was built specifically so that POW labor could help with flood control and irrigation projects in the river valley. But when there were not enough materials to complete the project, the camp became a branch of Atlanta, and the number of POWs dramatically decreased.

In July 1944, the segregation of Nazis from anti-Nazis began in earnest, and Camp Indianola was selected to house pro-Nazi, noncommissioned officers. It once more became a base camp. Oddly, though, these non-coms were not from other Seventh Service Command camps but from the Ninth Service Command. These men were hard-core Nazis and possibly war criminals. By September 5, 1944, there were 906 of them in Indianola.[333]

At least 107 of those "agitators" had been shipped out of the camp in March 1945. Prisoners told Dr. Rudolph Fischer from the Legation of Switzerland that "the camp had improved a great deal." The U.S. War Department then implemented the Intellectual Diversion Program at the camp.[334]

Wolfgang Decker recorded his memories of arriving at Camp Indianola. After being greeted by the commanding officer, Decker remembers the commander saying, "You will be treated well...if you comply with camp regulations. Dinner at six...dismissed!" Decker wrote, "We cannot believe what we just heard. There must be a catch, a trap or something to happen later." But it wasn't a trap, of course, and that night, Decker was thrilled to discover good food and a warm bed.[335]

After the war with Germany ended, the camp was deactivated on August 1, 1945, and once again became a base camp of Atlanta. German prisoners worked at the nearby McCook Army Air Field and on farms. It was officially closed on January 16, 1946.[336] The Indianola Historical Society has a nice collection of information on the camp.

GRAND ISLAND

Leo B. Stuhr, president of the county Non-Stock Labor Association, was responsible for helping to organize a small branch camp at the Dodge School building on Division Street in Grand Island, located in Hall County about eighty-seven miles from Atlanta. It became home to around one hundred German POWs from Camp Atlanta. These men worked in construction and agriculture, but the school camp didn't last long. Lieutenant Colonel Smith from Camp Atlanta declared it a "fire trap," and it was closed.

Another camp opened in Grand Island at the Cornhusker Ordnance Plant, and this one was possibly (or quite probably) a violation of the

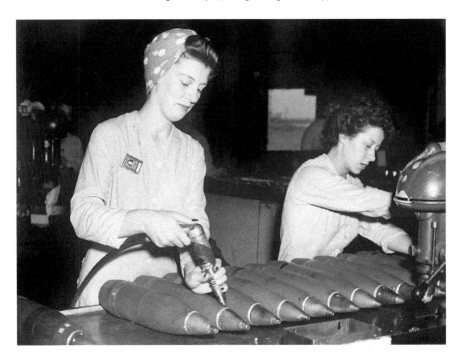

A female munitions employee works on a line of shells at the Cornhusker Ordnance Plant in Grand Island in 1944. POWs also handled shells here, which was against the Geneva Convention. *Wikimedia Commons.*

Geneva Convention. The camp, which held approximately 350 POWs, opened in October 1944 and was located a few hundred yards away from the plant. The official story was that the POWs were needed to help build the armament plant. But it went far deeper than that. The POWs helped manufacture bombs and shells, ostensibly for use against Germany.[337] The German POWs were "working on the construction of bomb load Line No. 4, the last line built at the plant."[338] It is unclear how this could *not* be a direct violation of the Geneva Convention.

The camp was specifically called the Cornhusker Labor Detachment, and its location on reports was given as Hall County, not Grand Island. The local media didn't report on the true nature of the camp, either. But one German POW, Sebastian Jocher, knew exactly how his work would impact the war:

> *We were sitting there in camp and a guy asked me—he was writing a letter home—and he said to me, "What should I write what I work for—what I'm doing here in America?"*
> *I said, "Write that you are working for an eraser company."*
> *"Eraser?" he asked.*
> *"Ja," I said. "An eraser company to wipe out German cities."*

Though the other POWs knew they were working at a munitions plant, they didn't "connect the dots," so to speak, until Johr's joke. Then the POWs went on strike, refusing to work. But no work meant no food. Eventually, a few days later, things were resolved, and the POWs went back to making bombs.[339]

OGALLALA

Only eighty-five German prisoners of war were at the Ogallala branch camp on January 31, 1945, when Maurice E. Perret visited. The POWs stayed at the Keith County fairgrounds. These men were employed in maintaining and repairing the Kingsley Dam, which was built in 1941. This dam created the now popular vacation destinations of Lake McConaughy and Lake Ogallala.

Unfortunately, the men at this camp didn't have much to do, according to Mr. Perret's report. They had no radio, no films to watch and the field next to their camp wasn't big enough for football. However, they did have a small library, there were plans to start English lessons and Camp Indianola was getting two film projectors, one of which would be used at Ogallala and other branch camps.[340]

BERTRAND

Downtown Bertrand, Nebraska, became home to ninety German POWs in early 1945. The vacant Andrew Johnson Store building was outfitted with enough showers and toilets to meet the qualifications to house POWs. The prisoners who worked at this branch camp became invaluable to the Bertrand community. Many harvested potatoes or worked in other agricultural pursuits, but many of them also worked for local businesses. Painting, fixing buildings, doing carpentry work and other odd jobs kept the POWs busy. Since the POWs at Bertrand had been selected for their "trustworthiness and general abilities to get along with one another," only two guards were needed to supervise them. This also meant that employers who used POW labor were directly responsible for them.

But the available historical record has nothing but good things to say about this contingent of POW labor. The Osborn Potato Company of Holdrege sent the labor officer at Camp Atlanta a letter stating, "We are very happy to inform you that the duties of the prisoners of war were performed in a matter altogether satisfactory to us. The particular prisoners assigned to use were very willing to do the jobs as directed." This was only one of many complimentary letters on the men's work ethic.

Since the *Bertrand Herald* was located directly across the street from the POW building, it liked to report often on the men's activities. One news story reported on the odd jobs the men were performing around town: "These men were obviously experts in their trades when they were at home in Germany, and still have a pride in even more menial tasks here."

The POWs also had a pet that had survived processing in North Africa, America and even Atlanta. It was a small turtle. The prisoners had painted "PW" in large letters on his shell.[341]

PALISADE

On October 31, 1944, a small labor detachment from Camp Atlanta arrived in Palisade, a village in Hayes and Hitchcock Counties. Housed in former warehouses, including the Smith Building south of the Frenchman Valley Bank, 152 German POWs lived and worked here, harvesting corn in the nearby fields earning four cents per bushel. The POWs had a radio and a small library and occasionally played games at a neighboring sports field.[342]

During one winter, local resident Irene Wright remembers being "scared of Germans" but said that she recalled POWs building a snowman and a snowwoman "complete with bosoms." Though two soldiers from Palisade escaped, they were soon found in a nearby chicken coop on the Van Meter farm located near Hamlet.[343]

ELWOOD

Located in Gosper County, Nebraska, the tiny village of Elwood sits thirty-three miles northwest of Atlanta. The one hundred German POWs who were assigned to the Elwood camp renovated the Agricultural Hall building at the fairgrounds. The camp opened in October 1944, and the POWs worked in the agricultural sector, mostly picking corn.[344]

BENKELMAN

On May 26, 1944, the *Benkelman Post* reported that, after months of planning, the local POW camp was now housing German POWs. Forty-five of them were already hard at work on Dundy County farms. Grouped in crews of fifteen men, the POWs were laboring on the farms of Magnus Fries, Otto Becker and Chris Nordhausen and would continue down the list of farmers who had applied for labor.[345]

The Benkelman camp had been established expressly because of the critical labor shortage. The 1943 corn harvest hadn't yet been completed by the time of the camp's activation, even though the farmers around Benkelman had applied for labor in late fall of 1943.

The camp was 135 miles away from Atlanta and 9 miles north of Benkelman. Killing bull snakes and playing soccer were about the only off-duty activities the POWs did in the short time they were here. The camp's seven prefabricated buildings were built in a grassy meadow and relied on two generators for electricity.

FRANKLIN

Located about fifty miles from Atlanta, the Franklin camp was established on November 1, 1944, near the small town of Franklin. There were ninety-two German POWs housed here in a former Civilian Conservation Corps camp. For entertainment, the POWs like to play soccer or Ping-Pong, but they had no radios to listen to. Neither did they have any educational courses set up, although they did have around fifty books furnished by the Atlanta camp.

During his visit on January 24, 1945, Maurice E. Perret noted that the men were currently working on maintenance and repair work on the local farms. Earlier they had been involved in gathering corn. Perret also said the morale at the camp was "very good" and there were no complaints to speak of.[346]

However, two POWs, William Heinrich and George Viegenhorn, weren't too thrilled with their situation. They had escaped only two months before in November. The two managed to make it twenty miles before authorities found them three miles from Red Cloud, "hiding in a clump of weeds."[347]

HASTINGS

The citizens of Hastings, Nebraska, in Adams County were not thrilled at the prospect of a POW camp in their town. In fact, the city council called a special session on May 1, 1944, to address the petitions circulating throughout the town. The petition read, "Believing it not for the best interests of the citizens of Hastings that war prisoners be quartered within the city limits, the undersigned citizens and property owners request that your honorable body go on record as opposing quartering prisoners of war within the city limits."

Of course, the firms that had requested POW labor in the first place insisted they needed POW labor to keep the local plants operating. They'd followed the correct channels with the government. Thankfully, a suitable building was found for the prisoners in southwest Hastings, the former Standard Oil Bulk Plant at West B and Cameron. By May 29, sixty-five POWs came from Atlanta and started working in the three local plants—an agricultural implement company, the foundry and the brickyard—while additional prisoners worked within the camp itself.[348] Because of the work they did, the men here earned more than eighty cents a day.

The enclosure included a sports field, and the POWs enjoyed playing *faustball*. They also had a Ping-Pong set and two or three radios. In this camp, the POWs had forty-three *Soldantenbriefe* from the German government.[349]

Thanks to Howard Hong, the men had paints and supplies that would enable them to create art and enter it in the Atlanta intra-camp painting contest. Local townspeople let the POWs use a violin, accordion and organ while Hong also provided them with a mandolin and a guitar.[350]

KEARNEY

The former Kearney Military Academy was the home for approximately three hundred German POWs. Kearney was only thirty-five miles northeast of Atlanta. POWs were given quotas of work to fill each day, a system that apparently achieved better results from the men, according to branch commander Lieutenant A.Y. Napier.[351]

LEXINGTON

Lexington is about forty-seven miles from Atlanta, and during World War II, the Lexington Country Club on the Platte River was home to around one hundred German POWs. The manager of the Meyer Milling Company in Lexington, Otto Meyer, wanted to use POW labor at his alfalfa dehydrating plant. Most of them worked at the plant, but others worked at nearby farms. A former POW, Sebastian Jocher, recalled an amusing story of how, when the men forgot their lunches at the camp, Meyer let Jocher take his brand-new car back to the branch camp to pick up the food. "I wounded up going over that railroad track at a high rate of speed and suddenly on the other side was gravel!" he remembered. "I swerved from one side of the road to the other before I finally got stopped...A jeep came passing by toward me. Then he looked back and shook his head and went on his way."[352]

WEEPING WATER

Housed in the former Civilian Conservation Corps buildings, the Weeping Water branch camp was located approximately 210 miles from Camp Atlanta in Cass County, Nebraska, and owed its existence to Cass County extension agent Willard Waldo. It was activated on July 18, 1944, and was closer to Lincoln and Omaha than it was Atlanta.

Waldo had responded to his local farmers' urgent call for labor by putting in an application for a branch camp. "At first everyone thought their County Agent was crazy," Waldo remembered. "I wasn't too enthusiastic about it either, but I had to do something to help the farmers." At the old CCC location, two hundred prisoners lived and worked in agricultural jobs, including apple orchards in nearby Nebraska City and a rock quarry for the United States Corps of Engineers.

Vernon Duwe was a guard at the camp. "They were just a bunch of guys, just like we were," he remembered. "They didn't want to be here, but we got along real well."

Years later, Waldo's records revealed that "305 different farmers in the area used POWs at one time or another." The farmers paid a little over $47,000 to the government for prisoner of war labor. The camp was closed on October 1, 1945.[353]
.

HAYES CENTER

Hayes Center is located a little over one hundred miles from Atlanta in Hayes County. Longtime resident Gilbert Gigax remembers the POWs being housed in the town's local community center around 1944. "It was a long wooden building on the west side of Main Street," Gigax said. "In the back, by the alley, they built a fence to keep the POWs in." The guards lived in the basement of a nearby building. Every morning, Gigax remembers, the guards would take the POWs out to work in the fields.

As a child, Don Fagerstone recalls being scared to walk past the building that housed the POWs. He also remembers when a few prisoners escaped but were quickly captured. "They thought they could just walk away and be in another country," he said. Apparently some POWs still didn't understand just how big the United States really was.[354]

HEBRON

Though the branch camp at Hebron originated as a camp under Concordia, Kansas, it became part of the Atlanta camp system on August 1, 1944. Hebron was approximately 150 miles from Atlanta in Thayer County and had been home to a Civilian Conservation Corps camp. This was where around sixty POWs came to work in agricultural jobs. Some even worked at the Northwest Turkey Growers Association plant at Deshler.

As a liaison between the farmers and the POW camp, Thayer County Agricultural Extension Office representative Francis Wiedel stayed plenty busy. "The consensus among the area farmers was that the prisoners did work hard for them," Wiedel later recalled. He also commented on the German prisoners' puzzlement over American farming methods. "They wondered why we didn't use the road right-of-ways," he remembered. "They thought the land should have been farmed right up to the road. They never did see why crops were planted right up to the gravel roads."[355]

CONCLUSION

The history of the POW camps in Nebraska during World War II is a fascinating part of the state's legacy. For many Nebraskans, the enemy was literally brought to their front door. This phenomenon undoubtedly changed many people's ideas of who the enemy was. In reading their stories, it is obvious that many Nebraskans did not view the POWs who worked on their farms or ate in their kitchens as "evil Nazis." To them, they were ordinary men and very human.

But the truth was much more complicated than that, of course, as it often is.

The POWs held in Nebraska had an overwhelmingly positive experience. Nowhere in my research did I find a single instance of a man complaining about his imprisonment in the Cornhusker State. Instead, their comments were positive, some would even say glowing. The fact that many returned to Nebraska to start new lives speaks volumes. Other former POWs have returned again and again to revisit Nebraska. For them, their stay in Nebraska epitomized the state's motto: The Good Life.

This will not surprise Nebraskans. There is, after all, no place like Nebraska.

NOTES

Introduction

1. Lois Neeley, personal correspondence with author, August 7, 2013.
2. Arnold Krammer, *Nazi Prisoners of War in America* (Scarborough House: Stein and Day, 1979), xiii; http://www.prisonersinparadise.com/history.html (accessed January 12, 2013); Joseph Robert White, *Review of The Anguish of Surrender: Japanese POWs in World War II*, January 2007, http://www.h-net.org/reviews/showrev.php?id=12797.
3. Arthur Kruse, "Custody of Prisoners of War in the United States," *Military Engineer* 28, no. 244 (February 1946), 73.

Chapter 1:
Overview of the U.S. POW Camp System

4. Krammer, *Nazi Prisoners of War*, 2.
5. Arnold Krammer, "German Prisoners of War in the United States," *Military Affairs* 40, no. 2 (April 1976), 68.
6. Krammer, *Nazi Prisoners of War*, 26–27.
7. Ibid., 36.
8. Ibid.

9. Krammer, "German Prisoners of War in the United States," 68.

10. Major Maxwell S. McKnight, "The Employment of Prisoners of War in the United States," *International Labour Review* 50, no. 1 (July 1944), 50.

11. Kruse, "Custody of Prisoners of War," 72.

12. U.S. War Department, Seventh Service Command, "Handbook on Facilities of Posts, Camp and Stations," Seventh Service Command Publication, August 31, 1945, Camp Administration File, Fort Robinson Museum.

13. Krammer, *Nazi Prisoners of War*, 37–38.

14 Antonio Thompson, *Men in German Uniform: POWs in America during World War II* (Knoxville: University of Tennessee Press, 2010), 6.

15. Headquarters, Camp Scottsbluff PW Camp, "Application papers relating to transfer of Cedric Goedecke from Prisoner of War Camp, Scottsbluff," RG 389, Entry A1 457, File "Scottsbluff, Nebraska, Miscellaneous," National Archives (NA from now on).

16. Ibid.

17. Thompson, *Men in German Uniform*, 25.

18. Thomas R. Buecker, *Fort Robinson and the American Century, 1900–1948* (Lincoln: Nebraska State Historical Society, 2002), 112.

19. Ibid.

20. Headquarters, Fort Robinson PW Camp, "Guard Regulations: Prisoner of War Camp, Fort Robinson, Nebraska," Guard Regulations File, Fort Robinson Museum, 11.

21. Thompson, *Men in German Uniform*, 10–11.

22. Buecker, *Fort Robinson*, 113.

23. Dean B. Simmons, *Swords into Plowshares: Minnesota's POW Camps during World War II* (St. Paul: Cathedral Hill Books, 2000), 14–24.

24. Ibid., 11–13.

25. Ibid., 13–14.

26. McKnight, "The Employment of Prisoners of War in the United States," 52.

27. John Brown Mason, "German Prisoners of War in the United States," *American Journal of International Law* 39, no. 2 (April 1945), 208.

28. Krammer, *Nazi Prisoners of War*, 28.

29. Robert Devore, "Our Pampered War Prisoners," *Collier's*, October 14, 1944, 57.

30. "LIFE Visits a Prisoner-of-War Camp," *LIFE* 17, no. 20 (November 13, 1944): 121.

31. Cynthia Mayer, "German Ex-POWs Returning to U.S.," *Detroit Free Press*, November 26, 1992.

32. Judith Gansberg, *Stalag U.S.A.: The Remarkable Story of German POWs in America* (New York: Thomas Y. Crowell Company, 1977), 42.

33. Krammer, *Nazi Prisoners of War*, 40.
34. Recollections of Mr. Steve Sorok, unpublished, undated, POW File, Legacy of the Plains Museum.
35. Headquarters Army Service Forces, Office of the Provost Marshal General, "Field Service Camp Survey. February 12–13, 1945," Prisoners of War Special Projects Division, RG 389, Entry A1 459A, Camp Scottsbluff File, NA.
36. Major Paul A. Neuland, "Report on Field Service Visit to Prisoner of War Camp, Scottsbluff, Nebraska, 12–13 February 1945," March 1, 1945, Office of the Provost Marshal General, Prisoner of War Special Projects Division, RG 389, Camp Scottsbluff File, NA.
37. Krammer, *Nazi Prisoners of War*, 39–40.
38. Major Joseph W. Clautice, "Memo to Commanding General, Seventh Service Command, Omaha 2, Nebraska, Jan. 26, 1945," Prisoner of War Branch, Office of the Provost Marshal General, RG 389, Camp Scottsbluff File, NA.
39. Krammer, *Nazi Prisoners of War*, 114.
40. Ibid., 81.
41. For an excellent discussion of the POW Labor Program, see Arnold Krammer's *Nazis Prisoners of War in America*, chapter three.
42. Mason, "German Prisoners of War in the United States," 211.
43. Ibid., 212.
44. Krammer, *Nazi Prisoners of War*, 35–36.
45. Ibid., 87.
46. Krammer, "German Prisoners of War in the United States," 68.

CHAPTER 2:

NAZISM AND REEDUCATION IN THE POW CAMPS

47. Office of the Provost Marshal General, Special Projects Division, "Field Service Camp Survey: Prisoner of War Camp Spokesman," Camp Inspection Reports File, Fort Robinson Museum.
48. Thomas R. Buecker, "Nazi Influence at the Fort Robinson Prisoner of War Camp during World War II," *Nebraska History* (Spring 1992): 35.
49. Headquarters, Fort Robinson POW Camp, "Memo to Headquarters RE: Transfer of Prisoner of War, July 12, 1944"; U.S. War Department, Captured Personnel and Material Branch, Military Intelligence Service,

"Memo to Prisoner of War Division, Office of the Provost Marshal General, August 2, 1944 by Colonel Russell H. Sweet," all in Provost Marshal General Documents File, Fort Robinson Museum.

50. Headquarters, Fort Robinson POW Camp, "Memo to Headquarters RE: Transfer of German Prisoners of War, February 18, 1944, by Colonel Arthur C. Blain with attached letter from German Spokesman Harry Huenmoerder, also dated February 18, 1944"; Headquarters, Fort Robinson POW Camp, "Memo to Headquarters RE: Transfer of German Prisoner of War, February 22, 1944," all in Provost Marshal General Documents File, Fort Robinson Museum.

51. Krammer, *Nazi Prisoners of War*, 180–81.

52. Alfred Thompson, letter of March 5, 1946, Alfred Thompson Correspondence File, Fort Robinson Museum.

53. Ibid.

54. Gansberg, *Stalag U.S.A.*, 59.

55. Ron Robin, *The Barbed-Wire College: Reeducating German POWs in the United States during World War II* (Princeton, NJ: Princeton University Press, 1995), 22.

56. Ibid., 195.

57. Ibid.

58. Ibid.

59. Krammer, *Nazi Prisoners of War*, 62–63.

60. Ibid., 196.

61. Robin, *Barbed-Wire College*, 59.

62. Krammer, *Nazi Prisoners of War*, 197.

63. Arthur L. Smith Jr., *The War for the German Mind: Re-Educating Hitler's Soldiers* (Providence, RI: Berghahn Books, 1996), 67–69.

64. Krammer, *Nazi Prisoners of War*, 201.

65. Ibid., 60.

66. Gansberg, *Stalag U.S.A.*, 77.

67. Krammer, *Nazi Prisoners of War*, 206–7.

68. Ibid., 86.

69. Ibid.

70. Robin, *Barbed-Wire College*, 56.

71. Alfred Thompson, letter of January 30, 1946, Alfred Thompson Correspondence File, Fort Robinson Museum.

72. Headquarters Army Service Forces, Office of the Adjutant General, Washington, D.C., "Prisoner of War Special Projects Letter No. 16," Special Projects Letter File, Fort Robinson Museum.

73. Robin, *Barbed-Wire College*, 57.

74. Alfred Thompson, letter of February 19, 1946, Alfred Thompson Correspondence File, Fort Robinson Museum.
75. Ibid.
76. Robin, *Barbed-Wire College*, 47.

PART II: THE NEBRASKA CAMPS

77. Glenn Thompson, *Prisoners on the Plains: The German POW Camp at Atlanta* (Holdrege, NE: Phelps County Historical Society, 1993), 155.
78. Ralph Spencer, "Prisoners of War in Cheyenne County, 1943–1946," *Nebraska History* 63, no. 3 (1982): 438–49.
79. Thompson, *Prisoners on the Plains*, 236–37.
80. Buecker, *Fort Robinson*, 124.

CHAPTER 3: CAMP SCOTTSBLUFF

81. U.S. Army Engineer's Office, *Cross Roads* 9, no. 5 (May 1943): 13.
82. YMCA, "Report on a Visit to Prisoner of War Camp, Scottsbluff, Nebraska, July 29–30, 1944," RG 389, Camp Scottsbluff File, NA; YMCA, "Report to (*sic*) Visit to Prisoner of War Camp, Scottsbluff, Nebraska, July 1–2, 1945," Office of the Provost Marshal General, RG 389, Camp Scottsbluff File, NA.
83. H.J. Knoll, "Memorandum to Chief Prisoner of War Branch: Repot on Intellectual Diversion Program, Prisoner of War Camp, Scottsbluff, Nebraska, 24 January 1945," Inspection Reports, Office of the Provost Marshal General, RG 389, Camp Scottsbluff File, NA.
84. http://italianmonarchist.blogspot.com/2012/07/elite-italian-bersaglieri.html (accessed January 8, 2013).
85. M.W. Downle and Douglas Stanton, "Italians Taken in Africa War Interned at Scottsbluff Camp," *Star-Herald*, June 25, 1943.
86. Herb Hinman, personal recollections, undated, Joe Fairfield Papers, Legacy of the Plains Museum.
87. Joe Fairfield, "Notes and Reminisces on the Scottsbluff, Nebraska P.O.W. Camp," January 26, 1991, unpublished, Joe Fairfield Papers, Legacy of the Plains Museum.
88. Downle and Stanton, "Italians Taken in Africa War Interned at Scottsbluff Camp."

89. *Star-Herald*, "Prisoners of War Will Be Available for Work on Farm," July 25, 1943.
90. A.J. Williams, "Italian POWs Added Spice to Potato Harvest," *Reminisce Extra*, August 2001, 62.
91. Fairfield, "Notes and Reminisces on the Scottsbluff, Nebraska P.O.W. Camp."
92. Williams, "Italian POWs Added Spice to Potato Harvest."
93. Lieutenant Colonel George G. Lewis and Captain John Mewha, *History of Prisoner of War Utilization by the United States Army, 1776–1945*, Department of the Army pamphlet no. 20-213, 93-97.
94. Office of the Provost Marshal General, "Copy of Telegram to Hon. A.L. Miller from Fred M. Atteberry, President, Scottsbluff (*sic*) County Labor Inc., February 26, 1944"; A.L. Miller, letter to Major Smith, February 28, 1944; Office of the Provost Marshal General, "Letter from Horatio R. Rogers to A.L. Miller, House of Representatives, March 1, 1944," Office of the Provost Marshal General, all in RG 389, Camp Scottsbluff File, NA.
95. Lewis and Mewha, *History of Prisoner of War Utilization*, 100.
96. Office of the Provost Marshal General, "Letter from Horatio R. Rogers to A.L. Miller."
97. Ferruccio Piccolo, fascist letter written in March 1944, part of Transfer File, Office of the Provost Marshal General, RG 389, Camp Scottsbluff File, NA.
98. Captain Lloyd L. Wells, "Memorandum to Commanding Officer, Prisoners of War Camp, Scottsbluff, Nebraska. March 31, 1944," Office of the Provost Marshal General, RG 389, Camp Scottsbluff File, NA.
99. http://frontporchnewstexas.com/italianpows010612.htm (accessed August 18, 2013).
100. Douglas H. Stanton, "Germans in Prison Camp Here Taciturn and Cling to Military Bearing, Smiles Are Rare," *Star-Herald*, June 5, 1944.
101. Lowell A. Bangerter, translator, "Writings of German Prisoners of War in Wyoming: Poems and Essays by Rudolf Ritschel," *Journal of German American Studies* 14, no. 2 (1979): 95.
102. Michael Peterson, "A German POW Recalls Kindness of his Captors," *Star-Herald*, April 17, 1991.
103. Stanton, "Germans in Prison Camp Here Taciturn and Cling to Military Bearing, Smiles Are Rare."
104. M.W. Downle, "Germans Prisoners of War Here Resigned to Defeat of Reich, Turn to Religion in Time of Adversity," *Star-Herald*, February 3, 1945.

105. YMCA, "Report on a Visit to Prisoner of War Camp, Scottsbluff, Nebraska, July 29–30, 1944," RG 389, Camp Scottsbluff File, NA.

106. Herb Hinman, personal recollections, unpublished, undated, POW File, Legacy of the Plains Museum.

107. *Star-Herald*, "Labor Requests Exceed Total in Prisoner Bases," June 15, 1944.

108. Lois Neeley, personal correspondence with the author, August 7, 2013.

109. Peterson, "A German POW Recalls Kindness of His Captors."

110. Bangerter, translator, "Writings of German Prisoners of War in Wyoming: Poems and Essays by Rudolf Ritschel", 95.

111. Wilbert Ruppel, personal correspondence with the author, July 26, 2013.

112. Associated Press, "Nazi Prisoner Sheds Tears as Gets Fine Food in Farm Home," *Star-Herald*, July 26, 1944.

113. Hinman, personal recollections.

114. Mrs. E.B. Fairfield, "Reminisces about Scottsbluff POW Camp," February 26, 1978, Joe Fairfield Papers, Legacy of the Plains Museum.

115. Ibid.

116. Doris Steele, personal correspondence with author, July 21, 2013.

117. Downle and Stanton, "Italians Taken in Africa War Interned at Scottsbluff Camp."

118. Douglas Stanton, "Germans in Prison Camp Here Taciturn and Cling to Military Bearing, Smiles Are Rare."

119. YMCA, "Report on a Visit to Prisoner of War Camp, Scottsbluff, Nebraska, July 29–30, 1944."

120. Downle, "German Prisoners of War Here Resigned to Defeat of Reich, Turn to Religion in Time of Adversity."

121. Neuland, "Report on Field Service Visit to Prisoner of War Camp, Scottsbluff, Nebraska, 12–13 February 1945."

122. YMCA, "Report to (*sic*) Visit to Prisoner of War Camp, Scottsbluff, Nebraska, July 1–2, 1945," Inspection Reports, Office of the Provost Marshal General, RG 389, Camp Scottsbluff File, NA.

123. YMCA, "Report on a Visit to Prisoner of War Camp, Scottsbluff, Nebraska, July 29–30, 1944," Inspection Reports, Office of the Provost Marshal General, RG 389, Camp Scottsbluff File, NA.

124. Neuland, "Report on Field Service Visit to Prisoner of War Camp, Scottsbluff, Nebraska, 12–13 February 1945."

125. YMCA, "Report on Visit to Prisoner of War Camp, Scottsbluff, Nebraska, July 1–2, 1945," Inspection Reports, Office of the Provost Marshal General, RG 389, Camp Scottsbluff File, NA.

126. Stanton, "Germans in Prison Camp Here Taciturn and Cling to Military Bearing, Smiles Are Rare."

127. Howard Hong, "Film Excerpt: POW Camp Scottsbluff, Nebraska, Visited December 16–18, 1944," Inspection Reports, Office of the Provost Marshal General, RG 389, Camp Scottsbluff File, NA.

128. Steve Sorok, "Recollections of Mr. Steve Sorok," POW Camp File, Legacy of the Plains Museum.

129. YMCA, "Report on a Visit to Prisoner of War Camp, Scottsbluff, Nebraska, July 29–30, 1944."

130. Neuland, "Report on Field Service Visit to Prisoner of War Camp, Scottsbluff, Nebraska, 12–13 February 1945."

131. Ibid.

132. Stanton, "Germans in Prison Camp Here Taciturn and Cling to Military Bearing, Smiles Are Rare"; Knoll, "Memorandum to Chief Prisoner of War Branch: Report on Intellectual Diversion Program, Prisoner of War Camp, Scottsbluff, Nebraska, 24 January 1945."

133. YMCA, "Report on a Visit to Prisoner of War Camp, Scottsbluff, Nebraska, July 29–30, 1944."

134. Neuland, "Report on Field Service Visit to Prisoner of War Camp, Scottsbluff, Nebraska, 12–13 February 1945."

135. Ibid.

136. Knoll, "Memorandum to Chief Prisoner of War Branch: Repot on Intellectual Diversion Program, Prisoner of War Camp, Scottsbluff, Nebraska, 24 January 1945"; Neuland, "Report on Field Service Visit to Prisoner of War Camp, Scottsbluff, Nebraska, 12–13 February 1945."

137. Neuland, "Report on Field Service Visit to Prisoner of War Camp, Scottsbluff, Nebraska, 12–13 February 1945."

138. List of Books Ordered from Barnes and Noble, New York, Prisoner of War Special Projects Division, Office of the Provost Marshal General, RG 389, Camp Scottsbluff File, NA.

139. Stanton, "Germans in Prison Camp Here Taciturn and Cling to Military Bearing, Smiles Are Rare"; Downle, "German Prisoners of War Here Resigned to Defeat of Reich, Turn to Religion in Time of Adversity."

140. Knoll, "Memorandum to Chief Prisoner of War Branch: Report on Intellectual Diversion Program, Prisoner of War Camp, Scottsbluff, Nebraska, 24 January 1945."

141. Ibid.

142. Harold L. Browne, "Letter to General Electric Company", February 9, 1945. Prisoner of War Special Projects Division, Office of the Provost Marshal General, RG 389, Camp Scottsbluff File, NA.
143. Neuland, "Report on Field Service Visit to Prisoner of War Camp, Scottsbluff, Nebraska, 12–13 February 1945."
144. *Star-Herald*, "Farm Labor, Inc. Would Keep Germans Here to Labor in Beet and Potato Fields," January 9, 1946.
145. Ibid., "POW's in Process of Evacuation Here: Going to West Coast," January 19, 1946.
146. Fairfield, "Notes and Reminisces on the Scottsbluff P.O.W. Camp."
147. Carol Murphy, "Werner, Erika Prautzsch Announce Retirement," *Mitchell (NE) Index*, October 10, 2001.
148. Diana Sherman, "Italian POW Returns to Area to Revisit Past," *Star-Herald*, April 13, 1999.

CHAPTER 4: CAMP ATLANTA

149. Thompson, *Prisoners on the Plains*, 3.
150. Legation of Switzerland, "Camp Inspection Report, July 22, 1944 by Paul Schnyder," International Red Cross, Special War Projects Division, Camp Atlanta File, Nebraska Prairie Museum.
151. Legation of Switzerland, "Camp Inspection Report, May 5–6 by Charles C. Eberhardt," International Red Cross, Special War Projects Division, Camp Atlanta File, Nebraska Prairie Museum.
152. Thompson, *Prisoners on the Plains*, 3.
153. Legation of Switzerland, "Camp Inspection Report, May 5–6, by Charles C. Eberhardt."
154. Ibid.
155. Thompson, *Prisoners on the Plains*, 13.
156. Legation of Switzerland, "Visit to Prisoner of War Camp, Atlanta, Nebraska, May 5–6, 1944, by Werner Tobler and Charles C. Eberhardt," International Red Cross, Special War Projects Division, Camp Atlanta File, Nebraska Prairie Museum.
157. Thompson, *Prisoners on the Plains*, 15.
158. Major Paul A. Neuland, "Field Service Report on Visit to Prisoner of War Camp, Atlanta, Nebraska, on 12, 13 February 1945 by Captain Alexander Lakes," March 15, 1945, Office of the Provost Marshal General, Camp Atlanta File, Nebraska Prairie Museum.

159. Thompson, *Prisoners on the Plains*, 23–24, 30, 34.

160. Legation of Switzerland, "Visit to Prisoner of War Camp, Atlanta, Nebraska, May 5–6, 1944, by Werner Tobler and Charles C. Eberhardt."

161. Camp Atlanta Soldier Newsletter, November 1945, 21, Camp Atlanta Newsletter File, Nebraska Prairie Museum.

162. Thompson, *Prisoners on the Plains*, 32.

163. Legation of Switzerland, "Visit to Prisoner of War Camp, Atlanta, Nebraska, May 5–6, 1944, by Werner Tobler and Charles C. Eberhardt."

164. Legation of Switzerland, "Visit to Camp Atlanta by Mr. Paul Schnyder, July 22, 1944," International Red Cross, Special War Projects Division, Camp Atlanta File, Nebraska Prairie Museum.

165. Ibid.

166. Thompson, *Prisoners on the Plains*, 65–66.

167. Ibid., 72–73.

168. Ibid., 84–85.

169. Ibid., 84.

170. Ibid., 272.

171. Ibid., 43.

172. Ibid., 54.

173. Ibid., 55.

174. Ibid., 281.

175. Legation of Switzerland, "Visit to Prisoner of War Camp, Atlanta, Nebraska, May 5–6, 1944, by Werner Tobler and Charles C. Eberhardt."

176. YMCA, "Report of Visit to Prisoner of War Camp, Atlanta, Nebraska, February 24–25, 1944, by Howard Hong," Special War Projects Division Camp Atlanta, Nebraska Prairie Museum.

177. YMCA, "Report of Visit to Prisoner of War Camp, Atlanta, Nebraska with side-camps, August 9–17, 1945 by Sture Persson," Special War Projects Division, Camp Atlanta File, Nebraska Prairie Museum.

178. YMCA, "Report of Visit to Prisoner of War Camp, Atlanta, Nebraska, February 24–25, 1944, by Howard Hong."

179. YMCA, "Report of Visit to Prisoner of War Camp, Atlanta, Nebraska with side-camps by Sture Persson."

180. Office of the Provost Marshal General, "Prisoner of War Recreational and Educational Report, 1945," Special War Projects Division, Camp Atlanta File, Nebraska Prairie Museum.

181. Legation of Switzerland, "Visit to Prisoner of War Camp, Atlanta, Nebraska, May 5–6, 1944, by Werner Tobler and Charles C. Eberhardt."

182. Stockade, Prisoner of War Camp, Atlanta, "Pay for Orchestra and Theatre Groups," January 15, 1945, Camp Atlanta File, Nebraska Prairie Museum.
183. Camp Atlanta Soldier Newsletter, November 1945, 29. Soldier Newsletter File, Camp Atlanta File, Nebraska Prairie Museum.
184. Legation of Switzerland, "Visit to Camp Atlanta by Mr. Paul Schnyder, July 22, 1944."
185. YMCA, February 24–24, 1944 visit.
186. YMCA, July 27–28, 1944 visit.
187. Thompson, *Prisoners on the Plains*, 150–51.
188. Ibid., 283.
189. Ibid., 49–50.
190. Legation of Switzerland, "Visit to Prisoner of War Camp, Atlanta, Nebraska, May 5–6, 1944, by Werner Tobler and Charles C. Eberhardt."
191. YMCA, "Report of Visit to Prisoner of War Camp, Atlanta, Nebraska with side-camps, August 9–17, 1945, by Sture Persson."
192. Krammer, *Nazi Prisoners of War in America*, 53.
193. Camp Atlanta Soldier Newsletter, November 1945, 31.
194. Legation of Switzerland, "Visit to Prisoner of War Camp, Atlanta, Nebraska, May 5–6, 1944, by Werner Tobler and Charles C. Eberhardt."
195. Camp Atlanta Soldier Newsletter, November 1945, 31.
196. Office of the Provost Marshal General, "Intellectual Diversion Program, Camp Atlanta, Nebraska," By Dolph Stonehill, January 10, 1945. Special War Projects Division, Camp Atlanta File, Nebraska Prairie Museum.
197. Ibid.
198. Ibid.
199. Ibid.
200. Legation of Switzerland, "Visit to Prisoner of War Camp Atlanta, April 9–10, 1945, by Dr. Rudolph Fischer and Eldon F. Nelson, April 30, 1945," International Red Cross, Special War Projects Division, Camp Atlanta File, Nebraska Prairie Museum.
201. Office of the Provost Marshal General. L.A. Ellis, Letter to Commanding General, Seventh Service Command. "Participation of American Educational Institutions," Camp Atlanta, Nebraska, January 20, 1945, Camp Atlanta File, Nebraska Prairie Museum.
202. Neuland, "Field Service Report on Visit to Prisoner of War Camp, Atlanta, Nebraska, on 12, 13 February 1945, by Captain Alexander Lakes."
203. Office of the Provost Marshal General, K.O. Broady, Letter to Lieutenant Stonehill, February 2, 1945, Camp Atlanta File, Nebraska Prairie Museum.

204. Office of the Provost Marshal General, "Memo to Major Gemmill and General Bryan from Maxwell S. McKnight, April 9, 1945," Special Projects Division, Camp Atlanta File, Nebraska Prairie Museum.

205. Headquarters, Prisoner of War Camp, Atlanta, Nebraska. "Memo to Provost Marshal General's Branch Office from Dolph Stonehill, May 29, 1945." Special War Projects Division, Camp Atlanta File, Nebraska Prairie Museum.

206. Legation of Switzerland, "Visit to Prisoner of War Camp Atlanta, April 9–10, 1945, by Dr. Rudolph Fischer and Eldon F. Nelson, April 30, 1945."

207. Neuland, "Field Service Report on Visit to Prisoner of War Camp, Atlanta, Nebraska, on 12, 13 February 1945, by Captain Alexander Lakes."

208. Ibid.

209. Legation of Switzerland, "Report of Visit to Prisoner of War Camp, Atlanta, Nebraska by Dr. Rudolph Fisher and Eldon F. Nelson, April 9–10, 1945," International Red Cross, Special War Projects Division, Camp Atlanta File, Nebraska Prairie Museum.

210. U.S. Army, "Historical Monograph: Re-Education of Enemy Prisoners of War," November 1, 1945, Camp Atlanta File, Nebraska Prairie Museum.

211. Neuland, "Field Service Report on Visit to Prisoner of War Camp, Atlanta, Nebraska, on 12, 13 February 1945, by Captain Alexander Lakes"; Camp Atlanta Soldier Newsletter, November 1945, 31.

212. Legation of Switzerland, "Visit to Prisoner of War Camp, Atlanta, Nebraska, May 5–6, 1944, by Werner Tobler and Charles C. Eberhardt."

213. Neuland, "Field Service Report on Visit to Prisoner of War Camp, Atlanta, Nebraska, on 12, 13 February 1945, by Captain Alexander Lakes."

214. Ibid.

215. Camp Atlanta Soldier Newsletter, November 1945, 31.

216. Office of the Chief of Military History, Poll of German Prisoner of War Opinion, Office of the Provost Marshal General, Special War Projects Division, Camp Atlanta File, Nebraska Prairie Museum, 1–9.

217. Ibid., 15.

218. Thompson, *Prisoners on the Plains*, 255.

219. Harry G. Perkins, "German POW: Camp Atlanta Good," *Kearney Hub*, October 3, 2005.

220. Thompson, *Prisoners on the Plains*, 290–92.

221. Ibid., 265.

CHAPTER 5: FORT ROBINSON POW CAMP

222. Ibid., 101.

223. U.S. War Department, Seventh Service Command Publication, *Handbook on Facilities of Posts, Camps and Stations,* August 31, 1945, PW Camp Buildings File, Fort Robinson Museum, 220.

224. Buecker, *Fort Robinson,* 110.

225. YMCA, "Report on a Visit to Prisoner of War Camp. Fort Robinson, Nebraska. July 31, 1944 by Howard Hong," Inspection Reports File, Fort Robinson Museum.

226. Buecker, *Fort Robinson,* 123.

227. Ibid., 111–12.

228. Otto Ludwig, interview by Thomas R. Buecker, September 17, 1987, transcript, PW Interview File, Fort Robinson Museum.

229. Wolfgang Loesche, interview by Thomas R. Buecker, September 17, 1987, transcript, PW Interview File, Fort Robinson Museum.

230. Karl Deyhle, interview by Tom Buecker, August 27, 1987, transcript, PW Interview File, Fort Robinson, Museum.

231. Ibid.

232. Office of the Provost Marshal General, "Report of Visit to Camp, Prisoner of War Division, Provost Marshal General's Office, 19–21 December 1943," Camp Inspection Reports File, Fort Robinson Museum.

233. Buecker, *Fort Robinson,* 118.

234. Headquarters, Fort Robinson POW Camp, "Instructions for Persons Using PW Labor, April 29, 1945," Camp Administration File, Fort Robinson Museum.

235. U.S. War Department, Director of Service Installations Division, "Memo to Office of the Provost Marshal General RE: Prisoners of War at Fort Robinson, Nebraska, January 30, 1945," Camp Administration File, Fort Robinson Museum.

236. Legation of Switzerland, "Report of Visit to Prisoner of War Camp, Fort Robinson, Nebraska, June 21, 1944, by Verner Tobler," International Red Cross, Camp Inspection Reports File, Fort Robinson Museum.

237. ASF Inspection Report by Major Don L. Mace, March 1–9, 1945, Labor Reports/Work Assignments File, Fort Robinson Museum.

238. Report to Captain P.O. Peterson, Post Engineer, from Roscoe J. Craig, Foreman Fencing, Fort Robinson, Nebraska, March 30, 1945, Labor Reports/Work Assignments File, Fort Robinson Museum.

239. Confinement Order and Receipt, Army Service Forces, Fort Robinson, February 20, 1946, Labor Reports/Work Assignments File, Fort Robinson Museum.

240. Legation of Switzerland, "Report on Visit to Prisoner of War Camp, Fort Robinson, Nebraska, on June 21, 1944, by Mr. Verner Tobler, accompanied by Mr. Charles C. Eberhardt," International Red Cross, Camp Inspection File, Fort Robinson Museum.

241. Dave Cook, "Fort Robinson Prisoner of War Camp Revisited," *Crawford Clipper's Northwest Nebraska Post*, September 1987.

242. Legation of Switzerland, "Report on Visit to Prisoner of War Camp, Fort Robinson, Nebraska, on January 21, 22, and 23, 1944 by Luis Hortal," International Red Cross, Camp Inspection File, Fort Robinson Museum, 1–6.

243. YMCA, "Report on a Visit to Prisoner of War Camp, Fort Robinson, Nebraska, July 31, 1944, by Howard Hong."

244. YMCA, "Report on Visit to Prisoner of War Camp, Fort Robinson, Nebraska, January 24–25, 1945, by Howard Hong," Camp Inspection File, Fort Robinson Museum.

245. World Council of Churches, "Report of Visit to Prisoner of War Camp, Fort Robinson, Nebraska, June 28–30, 1945, by Carl Gustaf Almquist," Camp Inspection File, Fort Robinson Museum.

246. Letter to Tom Buecker from Wolfgang Dorschel, August 29, 1994, Religion File, Fort Robinson Museum.

247. Visit to Fort Robinson Camp by Mr. P. Schnyder, January 30, 1944, Camp Inspection File, Fort Robinson Museum, 2.

248. Legation of Switzerland, "Report on Visit to Prisoner of War Camp, Fort Robinson, Nebraska, on June 21, 1944, by Mr. Verner Tobler, accompanied by Mr. Charles C. Eberhardt."

249. Alfred A. Thompson, note on Varista program, May 27, 1988, Varista Programs File, Fort Robinson Museum.

250. YMCA, "Report on a Visit to Prisoner of War Camp Fort Robinson, Nebraska, July 31, 1944, by Howard Hong."

251. Buecker, *Fort Robinson*, 120.

252. Headquarters Army Service Forces, Office of the Adjutant General, Washington, D.C., "Prisoner of War Special Projects Letter No. 5." Special Projects Letter File, Fort Robinson Museum.

253. Karl Deyhle, interview by Tom Buecker, August 27, 1987, transcript, PW Interview File, Fort Robinson, Museum.

254. Legation of Switzerland, "Report on Visit to Prisoner of War Camp, Fort Robinson, Nebraska, on January 21, 22, and 23, 1944 by Luis Hortal."

255. Legation of Switzerland, "Report on Visit to prisoner of War Camp, Fort Robinson, Nebraska, on February 21–22, 1944, by Rudolph Fischer and William B. Norris, Jr.," International Red Cross, Camp Inspection File, Fort Robinson Museum.

256. YMCA, "Report on Visit to Prisoner of War Camp, Fort Robinson, Nebraska, January 24–25, 1945, by Howard Hong."

257. "Report on Intellectual Diversion Program, Prisoner of War Camp, Fort Robinson, Nebraska, 27 January 1945 by Major Helmut J. Knoll, Chief, PW Special Services Section," Special War Projects Division, Camp Inspection File, Fort Robinson Museum.

258. Legation of Switzerland, "Report on Visit to Prisoner of War Camp, Fort Robinson, Nebraska, on January 21, 22, and 23, 1944, by Luis Hortal."

259. Ibid., 14.

260. Thomas R. Buecker, *Fort Robinson and the American Century*, 122.

261. Ibid.

262. YMCA, "Report on a Visit to POW Camp, Fort Robinson, July 31, 1944, by Howard Hong."

263. Alfred Thompson, letter of February 13, 1945, Alfred Thompson Correspondence File, Fort Robinson Museum.

264. Wolfgang Dorschel, diary entry of September 13, 1944, manuscript, Wolfgang Dorschel File, Fort Robinson Museum.

265. Thompson, letter of February 13, 1945.

266. Dorschel, diary entries by date listed.

267. For a thorough study of the film program at Fort Robinson, please see Melissa Marsh, "Still the Old Marlene: Hollywood at the Fort Robinson Prisoner of War Camp," *Nebraska History* 86 (2005): 46–61.

268. Buecker, *Fort Robinson*, 124.

269. Alfred Thompson, letter of June 30, 1945, Alfred Thompson Correspondence File, Fort Robinson Museum.

270. Dorschel, diary entry of July 31, 1945.

271. Buecker, "Nazi Influence at the Fort Robinson Prisoner of War Camp during World War II," 39.

272. Buecker, *Fort Robinson*, 128–29.

273. Tena L. Cook, "Former German POWs Return to Fort Robinson," *Chadron Record*, September 13, 1991.

274. James Denny, "From the Sands of North Africa to the Pine Ridge of Nebraska," *Omaha World-Herald*, October 18, 1987.

Chapter 6:

Nazism and Reeducation at Fort Robinson

275. Alfred Thompson, letter of February 19, 1946, Alfred Thompson Correspondence File, Fort Robinson Museum.

276. Ibid.

277. Alfred Thompson, letter of February 19, 1946.

278. Ibid.

279. Legation of Switzerland, "Report on Visit to Prisoner of War Camp, Fort Robinson, Nebraska, on January 21, 22, and 23, 1944 by Luis Hortal," 3.

280. Alfred Thompson, letter of February 19, 1946.

281. Ibid.

282. Ibid.

283. Dr. John Neumaier, "Former German PWs and GI's Meet," *Northwest Nebraska Post*, October 1987.

284. Dorschel, diary entries of June 11, 1944, and June 24, 1944.

285. YMCA, "Report on a Visit to Prisoner of War Camp Fort Robinson, Nebraska, July 31, 1944 by Howard Hong."

286. YMCA, "Report on Visit to Prisoner of War Camp Fort Robinson, Nebraska, January 24–25, 1945, by Howard Hong."

287. Headquarters Army Service Forces, Office of the Adjutant General, Washington, D.C., "Prisoner of War Special Projects Letters No. 1," Special Projects Letters File, Fort Robinson Museum.

288. Alfred Thompson, letter of February 19, 1946, Alfred Thompson Correspondence File, Fort Robinson Museum.

289. Ibid., February 9, 1945.

290. Ibid., February 19, 1946.

291. Ibid., February 11, 1945.

292. Ibid.

293. Ibid., June 7, 1945.

294. Dorschel, diary entry of October 28, 1945.

295. Headquarters Army Service Forces, Office of the Adjutant General, Washington, D.C., "Prisoner of War Special Projects Letters No. 1," Special Projects Letters File, Fort Robinson Museum.

296. Thompson, letter of February 19, 1946.
297. Headquarters Army Service Forces, Office of the Adjutant General, Washington, D.C., "Prisoner of War Special Projects Letters, "German Books for Prisoner of War Camps, November 10, 1944," Special Projects Letters File, Fort Robinson Museum.
298. Alfred Thompson, letter of June 30, 1945.
299. Ibid., June 30, 1945, and February 19, 1946.
300. Ibid., July 28, 1945.
301. Ibid.
302. Ibid., July 27, 1945, and June 30, 1945.
303. Office of the Provost Marshal General, Special Projects Division, "Guide for Instructors: Course in American History," June 25, 1945, Camp Education Work File, Fort Robinson Museum.
304. Frances FitzGerald, *America Revised: History Schoolbooks in the Twentieth Century* (Boston: Little, Brown and Co., 1979), 56.
305. Robin, *Barbed-Wire College,* 95.
306. Ibid., 96.
307. Headquarters Army Service Forces, Office of the Adjutant General, Washington, D.C., "Prisoner of War Special Projects Letters No. 8. Special Projects Letters File, Fort Robinson Museum," Special Projects Letters File, Fort Robinson Museum. For a more detailed discussion of the books chosen for the New World books, see Ron Robin's *Barbed-Wire College,* 96–106.
308. Robin, *Barbed-Wire College,* 102–3.
309. Headquarters Army Service Forces, Headquarters Army Service Forces, Office of the Adjutant General, Washington, D.C., "Prisoner of War Special Projects Letters No. 4," Special Projects Letters File, Fort Robinson Museum.
310. Robin, *Barbed-Wire College,* 99–104.
311. Ibid., 105–6.
312. Office of the Provost Marshal General, Special Projects Division, "Guide for Instructors: Course in American History."
313. Ibid.
314. Ibid.
315. Ibid., lesson #11.
316. FitzGerald, *America Revised,* 109.
317. Krammer, *Nazi Prisoners of War,* 148–49.
318. Ibid., 161.
319. Dorschel, diary entry of June 20, 1945.

320. Alfred Thompson, letter of February 8, 1946, Alfred Thompson Correspondence File, Fort Robinson Museum.

CHAPTER 7: CAMP SCOTTSBLUFF BRANCH CAMPS

321. *Morrill Mail*, "Will Cooperate for Prisoner Employment," March 16, 1945.
322. *Bridgeport News Blade*, "Prisoners Now at Camp Here," June 7, 1945.
323. Author interview with Donna Blome Amateis, July 23, 2013, author's personal files.
324. Letter from Donna Hoffman Cowden, July 29, 2013, author's personal files.
325. Letter to Joe Fairfield from Donna Cranmore, April 8, 1978.
326. *Bridgeport News Blade*, "Prisoners Caught at Fort Morgan," July 12, 1945.
327. *Bayard Transcript*, "To Move Out," July 12, 1945.
328. *Mitchell Index*, "Great Western Dormitory Proposed as Side Camp in Mitchell," March 29, 1945; *Morrill Mail*, "Prisoners Are Available," July 6, 1945; *Mitchell Index*, "More Nationals, Prisoners to Work Fields Here," June 7, 1945; *Mitchell Index*, "Sugar Campaign Starts—Labor Need Critical," October 18, 1945; *Mitchell Index*, "Beet Crop About 65% Harvested," November 8, 1945; *Mitchell Index*, "PWs to Help in Piling Tops & Bean Threshing," November 15, 1945; *Mitchell Index*, "Last of German War Prisoners Taken from Camp Here—Go to Douglas, WYO," December 13, 1945.
329. *Lyman Leader*, "Resolution," March 15, 1945; *Mitchell Index*, "Name Committee to Study PW Camp Problems at Lyman," March 29, 1945; *Lyman Leader*, "Local POW Labor Camp to Be Increased to 300 Capacity," May 17, 1945; *Lyman Leader*, "POW Camp Being Moved Today," November 29, 1945.
330. http://www.nebraskahistory.org/publish/markers/texts/sioux_army_depot.htm (accessed December 15, 2013).
331. Ralph Spencer, "Prisoners of War in Cheyenne County, 1943–1946," *Nebraska History* 63, 1982: 438–49.

CHAPTER 8: CAMP ATLANTA BRANCH CAMPS

332. Legation of Switzerland, "Visit to Labor Detachment of Alma, Nebraska by Maurice E. Perret," International Red Cross, January 24, 1945; Major Paul Neuland, "Field Service Report on Visit to Prisoner

of War Camp, Alma, Nebraska, by Captain Alexander Lakes," Provost Marshal General, Special Projects Division, Nebraska Prairie Museum.

333. Thompson, *Prisoners on the Plains*, 156–58.

334. Legation of Switzerland, "Report on Visit to Prisoner of War Camp at Indianola, Nebraska, by Dr. Rudolph Fischer," International Red Cross. April 8, 1945, RG 389, Camp Indianola File, NA.

335. Wolfgang Decker, "Camp Indianola NE," date written unknown, part of letter written to Bill Downey, May 3, 2000, Bill Downey collection.

336. Thompson, *Prisoners on the Plains*, 158.

337. Ibid., 167–68.

338. Grand Island Visitor's Center Website, http://www.visitgrandisland. com/attractions-database/world-war-ii (accessed December 16, 2013).

339. Thompson, *Prisoners on the Plains*, 167–69.

340. Legation of Switzerland, "Visit to Prisoner of War Camp, Ogallala, Nebraska, January 31, 1945, by Maurice E. Perret," International Red Cross, RG 389, Camp Scottsbluff File, NA.

341. Thompson, *Prisoners on the Plains*, 181–82.

342. Legation of Switzerland, "Report of Visit to Prisoner of War Camp, Palisade, Nebraska by International Red Cross Committee, January 31, 1945," Camp Atlanta File, Nebraska Prairie Museum.

343. Connie Jo Discoe, "The Prisoners among Us: How Enemies Worked Together During World War II," *McCook Daily Gazette*, December 8, 2006, http://www.mccookgazette.com/story/1180630.html (accessed January 22, 2014).

344. Thompson, *Prisoners on the Plains*, 159.

345. http://genealogytrails.com/neb/dundy/history/germancamp.html (accessed December 16, 2013).

346. Legation of Switzerland, "Visit to Prisoner of War Camp, Work Detachment at Franklin, Nebraska by Maurice E. Perret," January 24, 1945, Camp Atlanta File, Nebraska Prairie Museum.

347. Thompson, *Prisoners on the Plains*, 111.

348. Ibid., 164.

349. Legation of Switzerland, "Visit to Prisoner of War Camp, Hastings, Nebraska Labor Detachment, by Maurice E. Perret," January 22, 1945, International Red Cross, Camp Atlanta File, Nebraska Prairie Museum.

350. YMCA, "Visit to Prisoner of War Camp, Hastings, Nebraska by Howard Hong, October 18, 1944," Camp Atlanta File, Nebraska Prairie Museum.

351. Thompson, *Prisoners on the Plains*, 156.

352. Ibid., 179–80.
353. Ibid., 177–79.
354. Author interview with Don Fagerstone, January 24, 2014; author interview with Gilbert Gigax, January 27, 2014.
355. Thompson, *Prisoners on the Plains*, 175–76.

INDEX

ABOUT THE AUTHOR

Nebraska native Melissa Amateis Marsh grew up on a farm near Bridgeport, Nebraska. She holds a BA in history from Chadron State College and an MA in history from the University of Nebraska–Lincoln. Her work has been published in *Nebraska History*, *America in WWII* and several historical encyclopedias. Marsh lives with her husband, daughter and the three research assistants, aka the cats, in Lincoln, Nebraska. Visit her at www.melissamarsh.net.

Printed in the USA
CPSIA information can be obtained
at www.ICGtesting.com
LVHW052030050124
768161LV00030B/1770